HATE THE WAR HONOR THE SOLDIER

Lessons from Vietnam

Robert M. Givens

ARCHWAY PUBLISHING

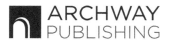

Archway Publishing books may be ordered through booksellers or by contacting:

Archway Publishing
1663 Liberty Drive
Bloomington, IN 47403
www.archwaypublishing.com
844-669-3957

ISBN: 978-1-4808-9522-5 (sc)
ISBN: 978-1-4808-9520-1 (hc)
ISBN: 978-1-4808-9521-8 (e)

Library of Congress Control Number: 2020916518

Print information available on the last page.

Archway Publishing rev. date: 11/25/2020

Dedicated to my wife

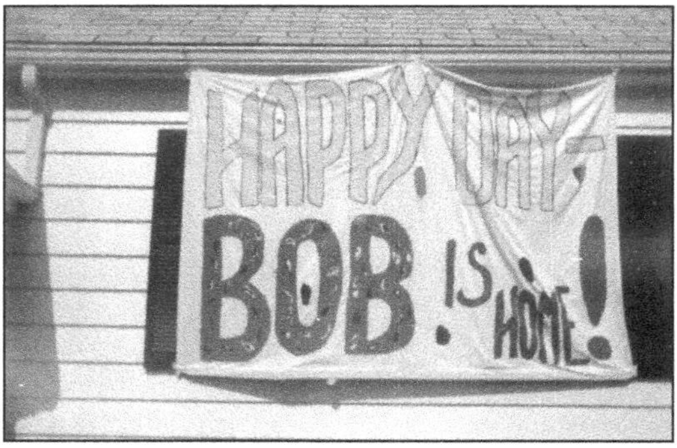

This book is dedicated to my wife Connie. She is an important part of every aspect of my life. We were married for only eighteen months when I was drafted. She faithfully wrote me three times a week and frequently sent me packages; she was my motivation to get back home even during my darkest days in Vietnam. Connie also is my biggest encourager. She loves that I enjoy writing even when my manuscripts take over portions of the house. Our lives are so entwined over fifty-three years of marriage that almost every episode in my life, including my time in Vietnam and my life after military service, involves the two of us. Therefore her perspective, which is often different from mine, broadens my thinking and makes the stories in the book more complete. And occasionally, she will wisely say to me, "You can't tell that story."

CONTENTS

Acknowledgements ix
Prologue xi
Introduction xv

One
A Nation in Turmoil 1

Two
Drafted into Service 15

Three
Welcome to the United States Army 26

Appendix Chapter 3 – Letters from Vietnam 37

Four
Off to War 59

Appendix Chapter 4 – Letters from Vietnam 79

Five
Completing My Tour of Duty 111

Appendix Chapter 5 – Letters from Vietnam 123

Six
Welcome Home Soldier 161

Seven
A Hunger for Healing 174

Eight
Life After Vietnam 200

Epilogue 219
Footnotes 221
Index of Names and Places 225

ACKNOWLEDGEMENTS

I would like to thank several people who helped and encouraged me in writing this book. My oldest friend, Allan Ferguson, was a paragon of literary criticism. Al is an accomplished author in his own right. In the midst of his busy speaking schedule, he took time to read each chapter with a professional eye not only to grammatical errors but also to content and substance. He also was forthright about challenging certain viewpoints—for example, the actions and mindset of protesters toward returning soldiers. His comments forced me to reflect thoughtfully on my attitude to insure I was being (reasonably) fair-minded rather than myopically reactionary. My favorite high school English teacher, the late Norman Stewart who was a stickler for grammatical correctness, would probably quip that it's a good thing I had someone like Al helping me in this regard.

I appreciate that my eldest daughter, Kierin, is perhaps my most outspoken critic. She is not satisfied with commenting "this chapter reads OK"; she is fearless about suggesting ways to make the book clearer and more expressive of my feelings. She is able to help me see how stories and themes can fit together to make them more personal and more poignant. She also is able to guide me through the inevitable periods of writer's block when words and ideas are not flowing easily. During one of those times, she wisely advised me to "just write." Don't be concerned with finishing a chapter or the context of a particular thought, just let the ideas and words flow paragraph by paragraph. As she is such a good writer herself, I am grateful for her creatively keen perception. I will want to read her memoirs whenever she decides to write them.

Finally, I am grateful to my buddies from my infantry company in

Vietnam during my time in country, 1969-1970. It's been over fifty years since I have seen these guys. We all did our best to protect each other during our time together and, as a result, we are forever united as fellow soldiers and friends. I also am indebted to the Vietnam veterans who took time to complete a personal Vietnam questionnaire for me. Some, like Bob Yantzie, served with me; others, like my lifelong friend, Dave Bradley, served in a different unit.

Other books by this author:
Heir to the Kingdom: Memoirs of Robert M. Givens

Typeface used are from the Monotype Libraries: Book Antigua (text), Segoe UI Semibold (internal book headlines), Segoe Print (introductions to the handwritten letters from Vietnam and Bible passages), Givens Antigua Pro Black (cover and introductory headlines).

PROLOGUE

I bought the hat at an Army Surplus and antique store in Naples, Florida, in early 2016. Nothing about this baseball style, navy blue cap was particularly distinguishing except that it displayed the American and South Vietnamese flags with the words "Vietnam Veteran" embroidered on the front. I had never previously worn anything advertising myself as a Vietnam veteran. I liked the looks of it and for $6.95 it would protect my bald scalp from the scorching Florida sun.

Then strange things started happening. The hat identifying me as a veteran drew attention. Every day I wore the hat around my Southwest Florida community someone would say to me, "Thank you for your service." In stores and even on the beach remarks were made, "I see you're a veteran. Thanks for your service." Some people just nodded at me with a knowing smile.

The service manager at my local car dealership said, "Did you know that as a veteran you're eligible for a 10% discount on your car maintenance?" A number of South Florida restaurants offer a free lunch for veterans on Veteran's Day. The waiter at my local TGIF Friday's Restaurant now recognizes me and anticipates my coming in every year to get a free cheeseburger meal. I was surprised to learn we could receive 10% off on a new washer/dryer combo from Lowe's. They needed to see a copy of my DD214 document to receive the discount. They must not regard the hat as an official military document. I carry a photo of this document with me now for the few occasions when people appreciate my service but need more formal verification.

I flew from Boston to Fort Myers the morning of Veteran's Day 2016. Jet Blue Airlines announced they were honoring veterans this day and would like any veterans to be the first to board the plane. Two of us moved forward to board as other passengers standing in line broke into applause. In Florida later that day, I received a free Apple Pie from Dolly's, one of my favorite lunch places, and a free car wash from Bonita Bubbles in my community of Bonita Springs.

I must admit I never saw this kind of reaction coming—either from others reaction to my Vietnam service or even my own reaction. In a Pavlovian sort of way, the more I wore the hat the more recognition I received, so I ended up wearing the hat all the time. I was genuinely surprised at such friendly, positive responses. Wear this hat at the Vietnam Memorial Wall, as I did in 2018, and it seemed like every school kid waited in line to shake my hand and offer a word of thanks.

How could this be? Some days I would challenge myself to see if I might get through one afternoon or day without being thanked. This kind of disregard almost never happened in Florida and even in the tougher Boston environment it was unusual. People were quick to say simply and respectfully "Thanks for your service."

It took me some time to get accustomed to receiving this recognition. I had lived forty-five years without advertising my Vietnam experience and generally avoiding those interactions. I didn't think it mattered to most people. Sure, many colleagues knew I served in Vietnam but very few asked me about it. In all those years only a handful ever said thank you. One exception was a friend at work, Dave McCarthy, who every Veteran's Day for over twenty years has sent me a thank you note or email for my service. But now, with this self-identifying hat, I was getting much broader positive reinforcement and, frankly, enjoying the recognition and the feelings of pride that accompanied the accolades.

The times have changed dramatically since 1970; people's attitudes also have changed. So many have forgotten what our country went through in this time. Some have mellowed with time. Others are just too young to remember anything about the period. As I began to casually engage in conversations about the Vietnam era, I was amazed how most people (certainly under age fifty-five) knew nothing firsthand about the war in Vietnam or about the turmoil in our streets. They simply lumped this conflict together with other major twentieth century wars; street and college rebellions were a hazy, forgotten history lesson.

I decided it was time to remind people about the Vietnam War and the devastations of that war not just on the soldier (though devastating it was) but also on the people in our country reacting to the war. For these participants, the war was intensely personal. This is my story as a twenty-four-year-old drafted, combat veteran—and it is intensely personal—with letters written to my wife that reflect my heart, my fears, and my dreams.

Wars are serious business—lives are tragically lost, lives are permanently scarred, leaders emerge, leaders fail, countries are ripped apart, countries are healed. The Vietnam War caused all of those issues and emotions and, as a result, we have lessons that should be learned.

Robert M. Givens
May, 2020

INTRODUCTION

I am a Vietnam veteran. I first saw the Vietnam Memorial Wall in 1986 on a family vacation to our nation's capital. It had been over fifteen years since my wife, Connie, and I had been in Washington D.C. and our young teen daughters, Kierin and Stephanie, had never been there. The wall was dedicated in 1982, so this visit would be my first opportunity to see it. The trip had been planned around stops at the usual places—the Smithsonian Museum, the White House, Ford's Theater, and the Washington and Lincoln Memorials. We scheduled the Vietnam Memorial Wall for a brief walk-by almost as an afterthought.

Even though I was a Vietnam veteran, I rarely spoke to anyone, including my family, about the war or my experiences in combat. I had no expectation that this memorial would be of anything but passing interest to me. There certainly was no desire to re-kindle or re-live my Vietnam experiences that were pretty well packed away in my memory. Over the years, I had seen many memorials to soldiers displayed around the country. Each memorial was mildly interesting to me as someone who cared about United States history—figures of soldiers from the many wars including Revolutionary, Civil, WWI, WWII and Korea. The Vietnam Memorial Wall, as it turned out, would be different.

I was unprepared for my strong visceral response when I gazed at the reflective, black granite panels of the wall engraved with names of over fifty-eight thousand soldiers killed in the Vietnam War. At first impression, just the simple dignity of this monument struck me. As I approached the wall, everything around me began moving in slow motion as if I was entering some sort of spiritual sanctuary. There was a sense of calmness and tranquility without a trace of apprehension in me or others around me.

Moving closer, I noticed people's voices grew respectfully more quiet—some were whispering, some were laying flowers at the base, some had heads bowed and were praying. Then I reached out my hand and touched the engraved name of my childhood friend, Steve Bangert. I immediately teared up and then began to weep over this emotional reunion. My girls were surprised because only once before, at the notification of my mother's death, had they seen their father cry. Instinctively and lovingly they reached out their hands to gently touch and console me. After a few moments they asked, "Who was Steve?"

I told them about Steve, my close childhood friend. We knew each other since before first grade from St. John's Episcopal Church in Decatur, Illinois, where we grew up. Steve and I were the two holy terrors of the church, but our antics were fun-loving and mostly harmless. The adults generally gave us plenty of leeway and fully embraced and encouraged us. The girls all liked us and flirted with us. Steve and I were in the choir together, we were the two head acolytes, we played on the church basketball team, we attended church camp in the summer, and we hung out together particularly on Sundays. We were good friends. I returned to Decatur from graduate school at Indiana University in March 1967 to attend Steve's funeral. Steve was a proud Marine, twenty-two years old and the first person I knew who had been killed in the Vietnam War. There would be others.

Bob Givens, May, 2020

ONE

A Nation in Turmoil

Fighting Two Wars

The decade of the 1960s was a time of momentous societal change and unparalleled citizen unrest in the United States. The primary driving force behind this unrest was our government's engagement with Vietnam, a small country in Southeast Asia divided between democracy and communism. In the early years of the decade, we supplied only technical support advisors to this small country. That situation changed in 1965 when we began sending armed military troops to fight in South Vietnam against the Communist regime from North Vietnam. By the end of the decade, we had sent more than five-hundred thousand troops to fight in this small nation. [1] Our country became bitterly divided over the conduct and effects of this military action. The opposition became so fierce that the war was actually being fought on two fronts—the fields of Vietnam and the streets of our own cities. No war had elicited such a massively hostile response from its citizens since the Civil War had ended almost one-hundred years prior.

During this period, our country became a boiling cauldron of virulent public outbursts with demonstrations over long-established values, racial strife, and the escalating Vietnam War. This period was like the month of March in reverse, coming in calmly as the Kennedy Camelot decade with hopes and opportunistic dreams, and exiting fourteen years later with the first and only resignation of a president of the United States. We became a nation not merely divided by political differences, but one formatively engaged in unresolved turmoil and premeditated violence.

For those of us who were living in the 1960s, we didn't see it coming. After the end of the Korean War, the decade of the fifties was a time of relative tranquility. This period was characterized by a burgeoning middle class of close-knit, traditional families with strong community ties and regular attendance at church or synagogue. Outside the amoral abyss of Hollywood, divorce was unusual in most communities, and divorcees and single-parent families were often shunned by their peers. "People know their place" were accepted code words that indicated our country was more stratified and segregated than most people understood or chose to believe. The fifties were characterized by idealized, white-dominated, middle-class oriented television shows such as *Father Knows Best, Leave it to Beaver, and The Mickey Mouse Club.*

Despite the concern over a cold war with Russia, two wars had been fought and won, allowing a general sense of comfort and well-being to pervade our country. Although more people lived in the cities than the country, much of America was still a rural-based, communal society. General Dwight D. Eisenhower (Ike), Supreme Commander of the Allied Forces in World War II, was elected president in 1952. This military hero seemingly knew how to run our country in peacetime as well as he had engineered our victories in two wars. After he ended the Korean War, President Eisenhower kept America at peace while he was able to spend ample time working on his favorite pastime, the sport of golf.

During a press conference in 1954, President Eisenhower first used the term "Falling Domino Theory" to describe the political ramifications of Vietnam falling to communism, [2] and that viewpoint came to define our strategy in Vietnam over the next ten years. This theory posited that one country falling to communism would set off a domino-like reaction that would topple surrounding countries. Presidents Kennedy and Johnson both used this theory to justify economic and technical assistance to South Vietnam in the early 1960s and later military intervention in 1965.

In one of his most notable non-military accomplishments, President

Eisenhower signed a bill in 1956 to build a forty-one-thousand-mile system of interstate highways across our nation, allowing vehicles to travel coast to coast and border to border without encountering a stop light. As a highly successful military general, Eisenhower understood better than most the harmful consequences of war, and he kept America away from such conflicts.

President John Fitzgerald Kennedy (JFK)

Exit the fifties, and enter the sixties. Our nation was never more hopeful than when electing its most engaging and charismatic president in John Fitzgerald Kennedy (JFK) and embracing his charming, sophisticated wife, Jacqueline Bouvier Kennedy. JFK was the first president born in the twentieth century and, at age forty-three, the youngest person ever elected president. The media coined the term "the Camelot White House" after the magical musical about a mythical place built on lofty principles and ideals. JFK inspired us to be a country that dreamed big dreams, that fought against injustice, and that would put a man on the moon in the decade. In his 1961 inaugural address Kennedy proclaimed the following:

> Since this country was founded, each generation of Americans has been summoned to give testimony to its national loyalty. The graves of young Americans who answered the call to service surround the globe.
>
> Now the trumpet summons us again—not as a call to bear arms, though arms we need—not as a call to battle, though embattled we are—but a call to bear the burden of a long twilight struggle, year in and year out, "rejoicing in hope, patient in tribulation"—a struggle against the common enemies of man: tyranny, poverty, disease and war itself....
>
> Will you join us in that historic effort? In the long history of the world only a few generations have been granted the

> role of defending freedom in its hour of maximum danger. I do not shrink from this responsibility—I welcome it. I do not believe that any of us would exchange places with any other people or any other generation. The energy, the faith, the devotion, which we bring to this endeavor, will light our country and all who serve it—and the glow from that fire can truly light the world.
>
> And so, my fellow Americans: ask not what your country can do for you—ask what you can do for your country? My fellow citizens of the world; ask not what America will do for you, but what together we can do for the freedom of man? [3]

We loved President Kennedy, his enchanting wife, and his two young children. We loved his youthful idealism; we had almost unbridled hope in his vision for the United States as a country of unequaled opportunity and global responsibility. The sixties, led by this man of stature, gravitas, and intellectually appealing humor, began with unbounded hope and optimism. He had quickly grown beyond his role as the face of America to become a respected world leader. But sadly, everyone who was over the age of ten on that fateful November day in 1963, vividly remembers the horrendous shooting death of this beloved president. Everyone of this age can readily answer the question, "Where were you on November 22, 1963?" (I was leaving my organic chemistry class as a sophomore at Millikin University in Decatur, Illinois when I heard the news.) In an improbable and tragic instant, the hopes personified by this youthful American hero were stolen from us. The nation and the world mourned the loss of this formidable American leader. How could he be taken from us so ruthlessly and quickly? Our tranquility, our dreams, and the trust we felt for our leaders were shattered.

Post-Kennedy Period

The post-Kennedy period beginning in 1964, and continuing for almost ten years, was the start of our nation in turmoil, a time unlike anything the country had ever experienced since we were at war with ourselves during Abraham Lincoln's presidency. Volumes have been written about the cultural and societal changes that defined our country during the 1960s after President Kennedy's death. Cultural changes and anti-government attitudes blossomed that couldn't have been imagined in the 1950s. One of the transforming phenomena of this period was student unrest on campuses around the country, starting in 1964 with the "Free Speech Movement" at the University of California, Berkeley and promulgated by a number of other groups, such as Students for a Democratic Society (SDS) and the Student Non-Violent Coordinating Committee (SNCC). By 1966, hostile, often violent protests began in earnest on college campuses around the country. Demonstrations were organized on issues such as racial inequality, social injustice, women's rights, sexual freedom, and more. But the catalyst for the most vocal campus demonstrations was the expanding war in Vietnam. Thousands of students at universities large and small participated in these gatherings of angry students; American flags and draft cards typically were burned in symbolic defiance of the country's involvement in what was becoming a hugely unpopular war.

In 1960, only a few Americans had ever heard of Vietnam, and fewer still could locate the country on a world map. Under directions from President Kennedy, the United States had begun sending non-combat advisers into this remote country. President Lyndon Baines Johnson, Kennedy's successor, continued that same philosophy and practice. Still, by mid-1964, only about twenty thousand US military personnel were in Vietnam, mostly serving in administrative capacities. [4]

The Gulf of Tonkin Incident in August 1964 was the catalyst for increasing American military involvement. This somewhat controversial incident based on flawed intelligence involved one of our Naval destroyers (the USS *Maddox*) located in the Tonkin Gulf that allegedly was fired upon by three North Vietnamese Navy torpedo boats.[5] There were no casualties on the American side, and the property damage was minimal—only one bullet hole in the ship's frame. An alleged second attack two days later has been disputed by subsequently released documents. Nonetheless, President Johnson asked Congress to pass a resolution, called the Gulf of Tonkin Resolution, allowing him to send in combat troops and assist the South Vietnamese against North Vietnam's communist aggression. This resolution, passed by a margin of eighty-eight to two in the Senate, enabled the President to take military action and opened the floodgates of war in Southeast Asia.

President Johnson was running for re-election in 1964. Until the election, Johnson felt compelled to carry forward with Kennedy's plan of minimal US involvement and supporting Vietnam only with non-combat advisers. His Republican opponent for the presidency, Senator Barry Goldwater, was a military hawk who portrayed Johnson as indecisive and unwilling to take necessary bold military action in Vietnam. Just prior to the election, and with the Gulf of Tonkin incident having been blown out of proportion, Johnson had enough reasons to send in American troops. After Johnson won the election in November, 1964 (by a landslide margin), he was able to establish his own authority and strategy regarding the conflict. And shortly thereafter, in March 1965, he sent in the first combat troops, thirty-five hundred Marines who landed in Da Nang. It also was clear the war effort presented more of a personal and potential legacy issue to this president. He was quoted as telling one senator, "I won't be the architect of surrender." [6] He didn't want to be the first president to lose a war.

The Military Draft

After passage of the Gulf of Tonkin Resolution in August, 1964, and prior to sending in the first combat troops, President Johnson announced the re-institution of the military draft, an action that had not been invoked since the Korean War. This draft created a battleground that encompassed and inflamed most of the roiling issues of the day. Thousands of young men would become eligible to be involuntarily conscripted into military service to help build up the personnel needed to fight the growing controversial conflict in Vietnam. Our country would never be the same.

Based on the 1940 Selective Service Act, every male between the age of eighteen and twenty-five was required to be registered with their local draft board. They had to register within thirty days after reaching their eighteenth birthday. As a result, these men were locked into an active draft system that had been dormant since 1953. They essentially had an invisible tracking device attached to them that was monitored by the United States government. The government required these young men to inform their local draft board of every change in their status and contact information, including address, telephone number, and job or school. The draft boards were made up of local community members who evaluated a person's draft status and who had a quota of inductees they needed to deliver to the military (usually the Army.) Because the people on the draft boards were generally well-known in their communities and neighborhoods, they were subject to intense pressure regarding whom to call up and which of these men received some form of deferment. Therefore, and not surprisingly, these local boards were inherently biased and open to manipulation by the wealthy and powerful of the community.

Every life choice and personal decision for draft-eligible males during this 1965 buildup period of the Vietnam War was filtered through the crucible this decision/action would have on their draft status. For example, attending college was a common deferment for many, but there were obligatory federal stipulations. The Selective Service System required that a student be attending school full time and have passing grades. The pressure of this expanding war and whether to continue school, enlist, or find some other option to satisfy one's draft status was felt by every draft-age male. Tens of thousands of draft-eligible men fled to Canada for sanctuary and, until President Jimmy Carter pardoned them, lost their right to return to the United States without being prosecuted.

Some men refused to enter the military when called up, and a small percentage were sent to prison for one or two years. Men from wealthy families, and even middle-class families, often found ways to avoid active duty military service. Some used their family influence to get them preferential placement into Reserve or National Guard units that usually had long waiting lists of thousands of men. For example, George

W. Bush, our 43rd President, served in the Texas Air National Guard and was never called to serve in the war. At that time, the National Guard was seen as a way to avoid the draft. Others were able to get bogus medical exemptions from friend of the family doctors. The leading places to avoid military service were colleges, where students with the financial ability and intellectual acumen could stay for six years and generally avoid the draft. The result of these initiatives was that the great majority of draftees were poor, not highly educated, and from working-class families without the money or connections to keep them safely removed from the tentacles of the draft system.

After the Gulf of Tonkin Resolution, the draft floodgates were wide open. Tens of thousands of draftees each month were being sent to South Vietnam as the headcount soared from ten thousand in 1964 to five-hundred-forty thousand by 1969—and, the majority of these men were draftees.[7] In 1965, draftees were 21 percent of the combat force; the percentage increased to 70 percent in 1970. By 1970 the majority of war casualties were combat soldiers and the majority of them were draftees. [8]

Who were these men forced into active military service? Roughly 80 percent of those serving in Vietnam came from working-class and poor backgrounds.[9] In the book, "*The Wounded Generation,*" edited by A. H. Horne, the author says, "The draftees who fought and died in Vietnam were primarily society's losers, the same who got left behind in schools, jobs, and other forms of social competition."[10] A study by Badillo and Curry in 1998 showed that youths from low-income neighborhoods were three times as likely to die in Vietnam as youths from high-income neighborhoods.[11] On the other hand, men from elite Ivy League schools like Harvard or Yale, would usually admit they did not know one person from their school who either was drafted or who voluntarily enlisted. They were among the privileged elites who easily found ways to avoid getting dirty.

And so, by 1969, the confluence of anti-war activity and on-going aggressive military action had reached its peak. Over five-hundred thousand soldiers were fighting a bloody, unpopular war in Vietnam, and American society was in a massive state of unrest with as many people against the war as those who favored it. When President Richard M. Nixon was elected in 1968, he claimed to have a plan to end the war. His plan included shifting the ground fighting more to the South Vietnamese soldiers and increasing our bombing of the North Vietnam supply lines. Each of the American B-52 bomber planes carried one-hundred-eight bombs (weighing either five-hundred or seven-hundred-fifty pounds) they would drop on the enemy in a single flight. The bombings resulted in the death of many civilians and added fuel to the anti-war sentiment at home. Nixon's plan to end the war was ultimately unsuccessful. Although Nixon began the initial withdrawal of troops in June, 1969, our combat troops remained in Vietnam until 1973. The Paris Peace Accord signed in 1973 signaled the end of American soldiers fighting in Vietnam. However, that ceasefire ended in 1975 when the South Vietnamese government succumbed to the North Vietnamese military who took over the city of Saigon and eventually the entire country.

The War on the Streets

How had the war become so unpopular at home? A number of critical factors were at work to cause such domestic uprisings, including: (1) the involuntary draft, beginning in earnest in late 1965, was an unwelcome burden to every male age eighteen to twenty-five; (2) the visual representation of the Vietnam war through television and magazines was revealing and frightening to citizens watching at home (the first time these real-time war images had ever been available to the public); (3) innocent Vietnamese civilians were killed and stories of villagers being massacred were sickening to everyone (the My Lai Massacre was reported in 1968); (4) the loss of a growing number of American soldiers' lives; and (5) the duplicitous rhetoric from Presidents Johnson and Nixon and other government officials that became obvious to informed citizens.

By the mid-sixties, in addition to the growing number of anti-war protests, racial issues had become increasingly menacing. The August 1965 race riots in the Watts section of Los Angeles were one of the first of a series of big-city riots in the sixties. The riot was instigated by the police arrest of a young black man for reckless driving that quickly escalated into a battle between police and throngs of blacks from the neighboring area. Over six days, sixteen thousand police and National Guardsmen were called in to stop the rioting. Thirty-four civilians were killed, over one thousand were injured, almost three thousand five hundred arrested, and over one thousand buildings were damaged or destroyed. [12] A fifty square mile swath of Los Angeles was transformed into a combat zone during these six days.

Chicago was hit twice in 1968 by violent street protests. In March, after the murder of Dr. Martin Luther King Jr., Chicago's west side neighborhoods exploded with violence and looting. Thousands took to the streets looting and burning down entire buildings. Over two thousand fire fighters were battling the blazes and twenty-five hundred police officers were called to duty. All told two-hundred-sixty stores and businesses were destroyed and another seventy-two had to be razed in an area of less than one square mile. Nine people were killed.[13]

Later, in August of 1968, the Democratic party held their national convention in Chicago to select their presidential nominee. A number of anti-war groups, including Jerry Rubin and the Youth International Party (Yippies), David Dellinger and the National Mobilization Committee to End the War in Vietnam (MOBE), and Tom Hayden and the Students for a Democratic Society (SDS), vowed to disrupt the city and the convention with their anti-war demonstrations. In response to what Mayor Richard Daley saw as a threat to the city and his ironclad rule of order, he called up twelve thousand police officers, five thousand six hundred National Guardsmen, and five thousand Army troopers.[14] A curfew was set for 11:00 p.m. with orders to arrest any protesters on the streets after that hour. The clashes over several nights between the large numbers of police and soldiers armed with wooden batons, police dogs, and firearms and thousands of protesters resulted in total chaos and physical beatings. Over six-hundred people were arrested with many more injured during the week of protests. The action outside the Democratic party convention center was seen by millions of television viewers. Nothing showing such wide-spread violence on American streets had ever before been televised live. The American public was shocked—some by the aggressively violent police actions and others by the brazen unlawfulness of the protesters. A federal commission later put the bulk of the blame on the police, calling the event a "police riot." [15]

In October, 1969, the *Moratorium to End the War in Vietnam* was initiated by a group of political activists who were against the war, including people who had worked on Senator George McGovern's committee for United States President in 1968. [16] McGovern had vigorously opposed the war. These activists were successful in extending the protests from college campuses to mainstream American communities to show, in part at least, that "normal" people were also opposed to the war. On November 15, 1968, over five hundred thousand demonstrators descended on Washington D.C. As part of the protest, thousands of marchers walked silently down Pennsylvania Avenue toward the White House carrying placards with the names of an American soldier killed in the war. [17]

The shootings of unarmed students at Kent State University in early 1970 was the most tragic of the college protests and shocked the conscience of our nation, no matter on what side of the war debate a person stood. On May 4, 1970, young, inexperienced Ohio National Guardsmen were called in to quell a quickly-proliferating campus disturbance. When shouting and tensions mounted, twenty-eight of these guardsmen fired live rounds into crowds of protesting but unarmed students, killing four and wounding nine others, one of whom was paralyzed for life. [18] Our entire nation was shaken by these deaths. In days following the shootings, and while much of the nation mourned, over four-million students staged strikes as many colleges and even high schools were forced to close down for days, stretching into weeks for some. [19]

After Kent State, demonstrations intensified throughout the country in urban areas including San Francisco and our nation's capital. On May 10, bombs exploded in Washington D.C. and blew out windows in several office buildings (the Weathermen claimed responsibility), while over 100,000 people brought parts of the city to a standstill. [20] Thirty Reserve Officer Training Corp (ROTC) buildings around the country were burned or bombed during this timeframe. Violent clashes between police and students were commonplace. National Guard units were mobilized at over twenty campuses in sixteen states. Ray Price, Nixon's speechwriter, described the Washington demonstration, saying, "The city was an armed camp. The mobs were smashing windows, slashing tires, dragging parked cars into intersections ... That's not a student protest. That's a civil war." [21]

At this same time, the streets also were filled with women marching for Women's Equality. These demonstrations, impactful yet more peaceful than the anti-war protests, set the stage for the introduction in 1971 of the Equal Rights Amendment to the Constitution. Betty Friedan's 1963 book, *The Feminine Mystique,* challenged traditional female roles and stereotypes and helped bring these issues to America's attention. Friedan and other women like Gloria Steinem, author and publisher of the magazine, *Ms.*, became leaders of the Women's Liberation Movement that sought equal rights, equal opportunities, and greater personal freedom for women. On August 26, 1970, in New York City and several other cities around the country, there was a protest strike for equality by over fifty thousand women who also were recognizing the fiftieth anniversary of adoption of the nineteenth amendment, granting women the right to vote. [22]

The Reverend Dr. Martin Luther King Jr.

Another powerful force during the 1960s was Dr. Martin Luther King Jr. He brought the civil rights movement into national consciousness, leading civil rights marches around the country with his commanding presence and oratory and his philosophy of nonviolent civil disobedience. Dr. King brought forward the plight of the Negro (the term generally used for African Americans or people of color in the 1960s). He led marches, particularly throughout the South, decrying the deplorable treatment of people of color in our country. Throughout the 1960s, Martin Luther King became an eloquent spokesman and effective leader for an entire race and for many other fair-minded people. In August 1963, Dr. King delivered his most famous speech, entitled "I Have a Dream," to over two-hundred-fifty thousand civil rights supporters from the steps of the Lincoln Memorial in Washington, D.C. The speech was the first civil rights speech to be televised throughout the country and has been ranked by scholars in a 1999 poll as the greatest speech of the twentieth century. The closing lines of his speech, delivered in with his unique tone and cadence, were: [23]

> I have a dream that one day this nation will rise up and live out the true meaning of its creed; "We hold these truths to be self-evident, that all men are created equal."
>
> I have a dream that one day on the red hills of Georgia, the sons of former slaves and the sons of former slave owners will be able to sit down together at the table of brotherhood ...
>
> I have a dream that my four little children will one day live in a nation where they will not be judged by the color of their skin but by the content of their character ...
>
> I have a dream that one day every valley shall be exalted, and every hill and mountain shall be made low, the rough places will be made plain, and the crooked places will be made straight, and the glory of the Lord shall be revealed and all flesh shall see it together.
>
> This is our hope, and this is the faith that I go back to the South with.
>
> And so let freedom ring from the prodigious hilltops of New Hampshire. Let freedom ring from the mighty mountains of New York. Let freedom ring from the heightening Alleghenies in Pennsylvania. Let freedom ring from the snow-capped Rockies of Colorado. Let freedom ring from the curvaceous slopes of California ... From every mountainside, let freedom ring.
>
> And when this happens, and when we allow freedom to ring, when we let it ring from every village and every

> hamlet, from every state and every city, we will be able to speed up that day when *all* of God's children, black men and white men, Jews and Gentiles, Protestants and Catholics, will be able to join hands and sing in the words of the old Negro spiritual:
>
> *Free at last! Free at last!*
> *Thank God almighty, we are free at last!* [24]

Tragically only five years after the death of President Kennedy, Dr. King, a 1964 Nobel Peace Prize recipient, was assassinated by a deranged racist gunman in Memphis, Tennessee, on April 4, 1968. Dr. King was the pre-eminent leader in the civil rights movement of the 1960s; he had preached for racial equality and against violence his entire life. His death was another terrible and untimely loss for our country.

Dr. King was followed by a more militant string of people and organizations that did not follow his strict adherence to nonviolent civil disobedience. Groups like the Nation of Islam (led by Elijah Muhammad and then Malcom X) and the Black Panther Party (founded by Huey Newton and Bobby Seale) were raising awareness of and literally fighting in the streets for black power and for civil rights.

Dr. King, who originally supported the country's efforts in Vietnam, became critical of our involvement as the war dragged on and so many lives were being lost. In April 1967, at the Riverside Church in New York City, he gave his defining speech on the topic. In it he decried this country's war that largely was being fought by the poor and the marginalized, both black and white. [25] And, of course, he was right.

The Vietnam War was fought on two fronts—in the fields of this remote country and in the streets of America's cities. This war was unpopular at home and unwanted by many, who were willing to vigorously protest, destroy property, and battle armed police to fiercely express their anger. At the same time, the soldiers, mainly draftees, answered the country's call to serve and fought their battles in the fields of Vietnam. Our nation was in turmoil.

TWO

Drafted into Service

Growing up in Decatur, Illinois

In June, 1966, I graduated from Millikin University in my hometown of Decatur, Illinois. I had lived my entire life in this modest Midwest agricultural community and factory town of sixty thousand people in the heart of some of America's best farmland. Decatur is in Central Illinois surrounded by rich fields of soybeans, corn, sorghum with a healthy dose of pigs and chickens. Decatur was known by the self-proclaimed title of "Soybean Capital of the World." A.E Staley Manufacturing Company, the largest employer in town processed these grains and crops into everyday domestic products like corn goods, syrup, and household starches. Other factories in Decatur included Caterpillar heavy equipment, Firestone tires, and Mueller Company, a foundry for creating fire hydrants and other water distribution products.

Decatur was a stratified community. The doctors, lawyers, and business executives lived either on the pristine west side of town or the upscale east side around the main drinking and recreational water source, Lake Decatur. The factory workers, truck drivers, construction workers, and other blue-collar families did not have those living options. For the first eleven years of my life I lived on the west side of town, attended the best elementary school, and hobnobbed with kids from Decatur's socially elite families at South Side Country Club. My dad owned a highly successful construction business (C.J. Givens Roofing and Siding) that allowed him to employ numerous domestic workers, including a live-in maid, cleaning people, and outdoor maintenance people. Our family traveled frequently to large Midwest cities like St. Louis and Chicago where we attended theatrical shows and sports events. We even spent one winter at a rented home in Ft. Lauderdale, Florida, while my mother was recovering from a back operation. In fifth grade my picture was in the local newspaper as part of Miss Van Dyke's social dancing class held at the members-only Decatur Club. There were at least twenty grade schools in Decatur, but all of the students enrolled in this class were from Dennis School, my west side, upper class elementary school. We were living the "good life."

My whole world changed dramatically with my parents' nasty divorce in 1955. As part of the divorce settlement, my mother was awarded the construction business my father had started seventeen years prior. She was an intelligent woman and a bookkeeper by education, but she had no skills or training to run this kind of a tradesman's business. She filed for bankruptcy in 1956, and our comfortable lifestyle and living conditions quickly changed. Unlike today, bankruptcy and even divorce in the 1950s were unusual and only taken as a last resort for a person and family totally unable to meet their financial and social obligations. Our family was struggling financially and relationally, and, to make matters worse, we were ostracized by our former friends and neighbors. I saw the shallowness of these kinds of "social friendships" as very few of my mother's hundreds of country club friends bothered to continue any kind of caring relationship with her or our family after we moved out of the west side of town.

After the bankruptcy and over the next ten years, neither of my parents was able to work a steady job because of health reasons. My father had heart problems that prevented him from ever working again. My mother worked for a few years as a bookkeeper, but had to stop working and driving by 1962 (my senior year in high school) because of cataracts. Both of them struggled with alcohol problems. Consequently, money and housing became and remained constant problems for us along with ongoing health issues.

My world changed dramatically in those ten years from one of abundance and affluence to a below-the-poverty-line, single-parent family struggling to pay bills, including our monthly rent. Between 1956 and 1966, we lived in eight different rental properties. When we were unable to pay our monthly rent, we were given a thirty-day, legally-binding written notice to move or we would be evicted. I would phone my older brother and say, "Can you borrow your friend's pick-up truck tomorrow? We're being kicked out of another apartment." My brother and I got plenty of experience and were rather proud of ourselves that we could load up a borrowed truck and move everything into a new apartment in about three hours.

When I graduated high school in 1962, and by any economic measures, my mother and I were well below the government's poverty line. My brother was married by this time and trying to earn enough money with his rock band to begin raising a family, so he could not help us financially. My dad could not work and was unable to provide us any child support money. My mother received a small monthly disability payment. I worked some sort of paying job (or jobs) from the time I was thirteen until I graduated college. Because of a combination of our low-income level and my good scores on the ACT college entrance exams, I received a full scholarship to attend the University of Illinois sixty miles away in Champaign. However, the summer before I was to start at the university, my mom had cataract operations on both her eyes. In the 1960s, the recovery time from cataract operations was several months. I realized I needed to stay at home and attend my local school, Millikin University, and drive her to her doctors' appointments. And so I did.

The State of Illinois transferred my scholarship to Millikin University, but, because Millikin is a private school, the scholarship money only covered about half of my tuition. In addition, rent payments for our apartment were my responsibility. My mother's disability income basically paid for food and drink. So, throughout my four years at Millikin, I had to raise money for the remainder of my tuition, books, our rent, and any spending money I needed. We were definitely no longer living on the west side of town nor was our family welcomed at social events at the local country club, or anywhere else in town for that matter.

My transition from living the high lifestyle to barely scraping by month to month was perhaps different from most young people in Decatur. Make no mistake though, there were plenty of kids my age who lived a transitory, disability-check to disability-check existence. I certainly wasn't the only kid in this town working two to three jobs, going to school, and periodically getting evicted from a run-down apartment. After all, Decatur was basically a blue-collar town and I now was part of that environment. Also, no one caught in this lifestyle predicament, myself included, had a parent or a family friend who knew influential people who could keep us from being drafted. We were draft bait, prime targets—the kind of young men the military loved and pursued.

College

As I confidently strode across the platform in Decatur, Illinois, that June afternoon in 1966 to accept my college diploma, I realized I was the first in my immediate family to graduate college, and only the second person in my Givens-Berrick family line ever to complete a degree. I was proud of my accomplishments and how much I had achieved with no immediate family support. One exception to that scenario was my Chicago lawyer cousin, Norm Schmitz. Norm provided me a generous scholarship my last two years at Millikin that substantially reduced my tuition obligation so that I graduated with very little debt. At that graduation exercise, I was well aware of my situation regarding my military eligibility. Unless I could get some form of deferment, my military eligibility would change within thirty days from a student deferment (1-S) to the designation (1-A), available for military service. And, in 1966, "available for military service" meant you were headed for the draft and for Vietnam.

I had three options I was considering during my last few months at Millikin: (1) apply for medical school at the University of Illinois; (2) take a job with J.C. Penney Department Stores as a management trainee (I enjoyed selling clothes all four years of college working about thirty hours per week); and (3) attend graduate school at Indiana University (I.U.) in Higher Education. The University of Illinois wanted me to complete one year of graduate school before I could be considered for admission.

I had a flagging interest in medicine, hated the tedious science labs, and concluded I was not suited for this vocation. JC Penney offered me a position at $500 a month (livable money in 1966), but I figured without any deferment I would be drafted within six months. So, the logical choice was to attend Indiana University (which would get me a deferment), graduate in two years, then get a job working in college administration. I was unrealistically hopeful our military presence in Vietnam would be over by that time. I attended Indiana on a full assistantship, meaning all my room, board, tuition, and books were paid for plus I received a small monetary stipend ($300 per semester).

I loved my two years at Indiana University, a large, beautiful Big Ten campus with a great college atmosphere unlike anything I had previously experienced. The summer after my first year in grad school, I married Connie Richeson, my college sweetheart I had met at Millikin. Connie came from a highly-respected family in Rock Island, Illinois. Her father was a stalwart of the community and sr. vice-president of the local bank. Her family was strong, traditional, and stable; mine was shaky, single-parent, and chaotic. Even after I confessed my weird, nomadic lifestyle to Connie, she accepted all my baggage and we were married on August 19, 1967, in her hometown. Connie taught elementary school in the backwoods of Brown County, Indiana, while I enjoyed my final year of grad school.

While guys were fighting and dying in Vietnam, I was enjoying myself in school watching Big Ten athletics and keeping myself busy with interesting academic courses, sports activities like handball and tennis, and playing lots of bridge. I knew that obtaining a Master's Degree in Higher Education from Indiana University would assure me of getting a good job upon graduation in 1968. After one of my night classes several of us often would go to our local pub, called The Regulator, for drinks and conversation. I could not get Connie to go out on a school night with us because she said she was too tired from teaching all day and needed her rest. I made a major marital mistake when I questioned her stamina about being tired from a day of teaching and asked, "How hard can that be anyway?" She was (rightfully) furious with me. "Come and see," she challenged me. "You come and teach for just one afternoon, and I'll even let you choose the subjects." Many years later I was still licking my wounds from that *faux pas*. She was right. Teaching a group of fourth grade kids any subject, keeping the class under some reasonable control, and answering a million questions while multi-tasking with other duties the entire afternoon was not my idea of fun. Nor was it easy. OK, I was wrong and properly chastised.

Working at the University in Connecticut

Beginning in the fall of 1968, I was almost twenty-four years old and working my first full-time job after graduate school as an Assistant to the Dean of Students at the University of Connecticut (UConn). Connie was employed as an elementary school teacher in Tolland, Connecticut. We were born and bred Midwesterners; I had never even traveled to the East Coast, let alone New England, except for my job interview that spring. Oh, and I was not an experienced traveler. Using a ticket the school had sent me to fly to Hartford, Connecticut, I sat down in the first available seat I came to. It was a first-class seat. The plane was delayed a few minutes while the flight attendants checked everyone's tickets. I was more than slightly embarrassed when they rather dismissively told me I was in the wrong seat and had to move to the back of the plane. All eyes seemed to be glaring at me for causing this take-off delay as I unsuccessfully tried to sneak my way toward the rear of the plane. It was only my second time on a plane. I'm from Decatur, Illinois. How was I to know there was such a thing as first class?

Connie and I arrived in Storrs, Connecticut in July, 1968, pulling everything we owned in a rented U-Haul trailer. We both were hopeful that my job in a respected university and my relatively advanced age for a potential draftee, would enable me to avoid the ubiquitous military draft. But it was clear that the government was continuing to increase its military presence in Vietnam and needed more draftees to fill the quota. That ever-present tension was like the Sword of Damocles hanging over my head, as well as the heads of most eighteen to twenty-five-year old's. The realistic question was more "when" than "if."

When we arrived in Willimantic. Connecticut, at our newly rented one-bedroom, fully-furnished apartment, we tried to put aside concerns over the military draft. We had enough to worry about just moving to this strange part of the country, starting new jobs, and trying to make financial ends meet. We had stayed at a friend's apartment in Ohio (Jim and Marnie Parry) on the trip east because we couldn't afford the cost of a motel. After making our apartment rental deposit, we had two gas company credit cards and less than twenty dollars to our name. I would get an advance check in a few days from UConn; Connie wouldn't receive a check for another six weeks.

We needed to go to the grocery store, and, as we carried the few groceries we could afford to our car, we noticed a flyer attached to the windshield urging us to "Call for a demonstration of the miraculous Kirby vacuum cleaner and receive a free case of Coke." I snatched that flyer off the car and the minute we got home I called the number to set up an appointment. We had no money and certainly did not want to buy an expensive vacuum cleaner. But I was salivating over receiving a free case of Coca-Cola. Two nights later the Kirby salesman arrived at our door with this miracle cleaning machine and, more importantly, a case of Coke. I told Connie that we were throwing this guy out after fifteen minutes so I could get back to watching a football game. Lo and behold, two hours later we bought a $375 Kirby Vacuum Cleaner—no money down (obviously) and payments of twenty dollars a month for two years. This miracle machine came with every imaginable option including one that would allow us to paint the house. My colleagues at work, including my new boss, Bill Shimpf, got a hearty laugh over this story. It became the source for an endless array of good-natured jokes at work. "Did you drive that vacuum cleaner to work today?" Or, "Have you painted your apartment house recently with that expensive new tool you bought?"

We survived the early days at our new furnished apartment and gradually settled into a rhythm in New England. Everything about this part of the country was certainly different from the Midwest, including the language. We had to learn a new lingo—regular coffee was coffee with cream, a bubbler was a water fountain, a grinder was a sub sandwich. Boston, including all the cultural and sports activities of this major city, was less than a two-hour drive away. Bostonians had their own barely decipherable language. If a word ended in "a", like area, it was pronounced "air ee er." If a word ended in "er" like buster, it was pronounced "bustah." And a car was a "cah." Go figure.

Fall in New England with the multi-colored foliage and panoramic landscapes was more beautiful than anything we knew from the Midwest. We also loved that we could drive for an hour and be at the ocean on the Connecticut coast. We even learned how to boil and eat fresh, live lobster (not for the faint of heart). Smothered in "buttah", it was delicious. We were an easy drive away from the White Mountains of New Hampshire. We liked our jobs and particularly that we had some spendable income since, for the first time in our lives, we were bringing in two full-time paychecks. Life was good for this young, newly-married couple.

1968 was the height of opposition to the Vietnam War in the United States. There were over five-hundred thousand US troops in that country. Violent ant-war protests had erupted throughout the nation, and particularly at large college campuses like UConn. In most of these settings, the doves (those who demanded withdrawal from Vietnam) greatly outnumbered the hawks (those who wanted military victory.) In the midst of increasing tensions on campus, Dow Chemical, the maker of the harsh, disfiguring chemical agent Napalm, was looking to hire some qualified graduating seniors and announced they would begin recruiting interviews at our school. The protesting student groups (Students for a Democratic Society being the most forceful and violent) notified national media that they would not allow Dow to conduct these interviews at UConn. When the interview day arrived and national media like the *New York Times* were on site, the scene was set for some sort of violent confrontation.

UConn security forces asked for and received help from the Connecticut National Guard. As university administrators, we were put on alert and assigned to different tasks. I was to be an observer at the house on campus where the interviews were to occur. The square wooden house was completely surrounded by a porch with a white, wooden railing. The Connecticut National Guard positioned themselves shoulder to shoulder on the porch, helmets on with protective face masks and eighteen-inch long wooden batons held in front of them. Over one-thousand students were gathered around the building shouting and chanting in protest. I was in the crowd but clearly not one of the student protesters dressed in my suit and tie, standing thirty yards from the entrance to the house. The first student coming for an interview appeared and tried to make his way through a small path toward the entrance. He was hounded, shouted at, and physically jostled as he moved closer to the entrance. As he continued slowly to move forward, the pathway closed up and he was completely surrounded by protesters. The noise level increased ominously; pushing and shoving began in earnest. At that point I watched a university sociology professor standing twenty feet in front of me pick up a brick and throw it through a glass window in the house. Screaming, shouting, and total chaos ensued as protesters rushed the National Guardsmen on the porch. The Guardsmen began swinging their clubs and knocking over the advancing students. Blood was flowing. Never before had I witnessed such a violent and dangerous confrontation. I realized that I easily could become a target for the protesters so I turned and ran.

Many students were injured during that riot. The protesting crowd didn't disperse but moved away from the security force toward a small, two-story building that was the Office of the President. The president was not inside at the time. The protesters overran the building, forcing all university employees to leave. The rioting students took complete control of the building, even barricading the doors. I was standing alongside other university personnel watching the activity. Once the protesters moved inside the building, tempers had cooled somewhat and the atmosphere was not as dangerous as at the interview site. The president made the decision to stand down from using any security force to try to take back the building. He began talking calmly with the occupants trying to keep the situation from reigniting. He also wanted personal and confidential information contained inside to be safeguarded, so he asked if someone from the university staff could be admitted to ensure that documents were not compromised. The protesters agreed and shouted, "We'll take that one, he looks more like one of us than one of you." "That one" was me. I was twenty-three-years old, the same age or even younger than many of the grad students and "professional agitators" who were leading the protest. I spent most of the next two days as an observer in the President's Office Building. The students created a terrible mess in the office during the two-day takeover but with only modest physical damage and no destruction of personnel records.

The protesters departed the building when the national news media left the scene. Something didn't strike my small-town Midwestern values as exactly copacetic when events are being staged by the protesters for the convenience of the media. I also didn't like the fact that the FBI showed me photos from protests at other schools and asked me to identify students who participated in this disturbance. Some of the students were merely interested onlookers and I was concerned that the FBI seemed to be tracking everyone regardless of their role in the protest. Welcome to the real world where issues are more complex than sitting in a classroom.

Letter from the President of the United States

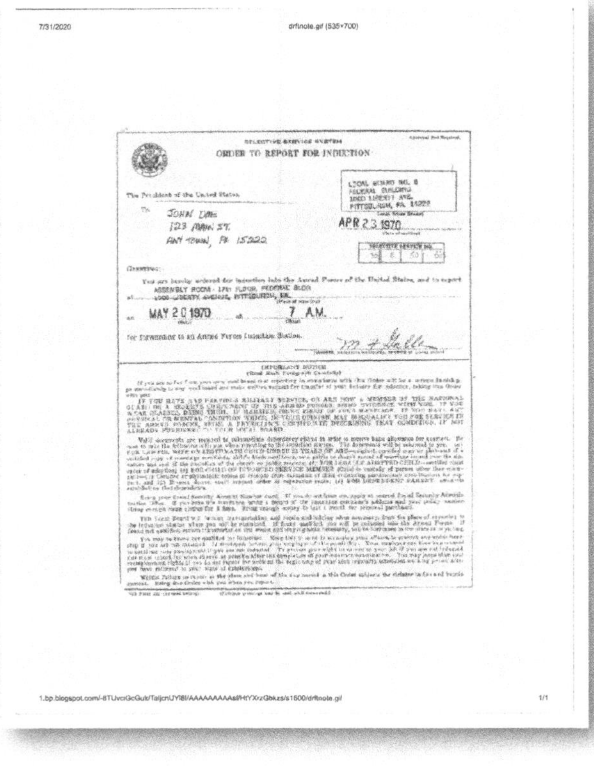

7/31/2020 drfinote.gif (535×700)

SELECTIVE SERVICE SYSTEM

ORDER TO REPORT FOR INDUCTION

LOCAL BOARD NO. 6
FEDERAL BUILDING
1000 LIBERTY AVE.
PITTSBURGH, PA. 15222

The President of the United States,

To JOHN DOE
123 MAIN ST.
ANY TOWN, PA 15222

APR 23 1970

GREETING:

You are hereby ordered for induction into the Armed Forces of the United States, and to report at ASSEMBLY ROOM - 17th FLOOR, FEDERAL BLDG 1000 LIBERTY AVENUE, PITTSBURGH, PA.

on MAY 20 1970 at 7 A.M.

for forwarding to an Armed Forces Induction Station.

IMPORTANT NOTICE

1.bp.blogspot.com/-8TUvciGcGuk/TaljcnUYI8I/AAAAAAAAAsI/HtYXrzGbkzs/s1600/drfinote.gif 1/1

In early February 1969 the sword fell. Connie was in tears when she phoned me at work. She read me the letter from the President of the United States saying, "Welcome to the United States Military"—I was drafted and ordered to report for a physical in Decatur, Illinois, on February 20, 1969. The Vice-President of Student Affairs had written a glowing letter on my behalf to my draft board asking them to allow me to continue my work at the university. He wrote that my work was critical to the operation of the university. The Army, and the Decatur draft board, needed bodies; that request was quickly and summarily rejected.

Connie was allowed by law to break her one-year teaching contract. She gave them a copy of my orders to report for a physical in St. Louis and the school released her from the obligation. She would live with her parents in Rock Island, Illinois and work as a substitute elementary school teacher the rest of that year. She taught in her own fourth-grade classroom for the next school year while I was in the service.

So, we re-attached a U-Haul trailer to our car packed with our meager belongings (our apartment came furnished with all the bedroom and living room furniture) and headed back to Illinois. Everything about our lives was instantly and dramatically changed. All of our plans had been upset by this induction letter from the government. Our new life and first professional jobs and careers in Connecticut were gone. Our dreams were put on hold indefinitely. Married for eighteen months, we would be separated from each other for who knows how long. I dreaded the thoughts of giving up all that I had worked so hard to achieve—leaving behind my young wife, postponing our desire to have children, interrupting my first full-time career job as a college administrator, abandoning my sixteen-years of education, enjoying some material benefits for the first time in my adult life—to move into an unknown, spartan, and dangerous existence for twenty-four months where someone else had control over most every aspect of my life. For the next two years, I would no longer be able to make any important life, marital, or vocational decisions. I was subject to the whims and the orders of the United States Army, and I never doubted that this time would be difficult.

— THREE —

Welcome to the United States Army

Army Training at Ft. Ord, California

Fifty men spent our first day in the Army together, reporting in at St. Louis and then being transported to Ft. Leonard Wood, Missouri, located in the middle of nowhere. We spent two nights there and were told this training fort was at capacity. About two-hundred new recruits boarded a plane the next day for Fort Ord on the beautiful Monterey Peninsula in Northern California. The month was February, so California in winter sounded much better than cold dreary central Missouri.

"Grab your duffel bags you low-life recruits," Top (the first sergeant) yelled at us the moment we got off the bus at Fort Ord at 8:00 a.m. "Duffel bag on your back, I want to see all of you low crawling across the pavement," he yelled. "Move it!" After a few more minutes of his shouting, Top got us into formation and changed to a toned-down friendlier voice. "Welcome to Fort Ord for your eight weeks of basic training," Top continued in a calmer voice. "Let me see the hands of any college graduates in this group." My hand went up with about twenty other guys—a big mistake. Top had the college graduates pull out their razors and dry shave. "Your big-time college degree don't mean nothin' here, boy," he shouted in our faces, returning to his drill sergeant voice. He also gave us a good description of where we fit in the Army hierarchy of personnel—"lower than whale [excrement] at the bottom of the ocean". Welcome to the United States Army, I thought. This experience will not be fun.

I was badly out of shape as I began my military training. I had gained thirty pounds since my wedding eighteen months earlier. A typical lunch for me working my first desk job at UConn was two Big Macs, large fries and a giant Coke. The first time we ran the mile during basic training we had on full gear and combat boots. My time for the mile on this uphill course was almost eleven minutes. Army training camp was geared, among other things, to get us into infantry-ready physical condition. At the end of our seventh week, we had to pass the Army Physical Training (PT) Test consisting of five different events. In anticipation of this rigorous training, I stopped smoking for the first time in almost six years. I was determined to do my best to max out this test.

My first letter to Connie was mailed after about ten days of Basic Training at Fort Ord, California. I enjoyed some of the classes, like hand-to-hand combat, but hated the Army mentality and regimen, including being assigned one full day to Kitchen Patrol (KP) peeling hundreds of potatoes. I treasured the letters I received from Connie.

Every morning before breakfast we ran in formation for two to three miles to the rhythmic cadence of our drill sergeants. (Below is one of the clean versions). When we weren't running, which wasn't often, we marched to some similar cadence.

(D.I. starts) "I don't know but I've been told (soldiers repeat)
Winter here gets really cold. (repeat)
We just march and run all day (repeat)
Cold don't hurt us any way (repeat)
Sound off (soldiers say 'one two')
Sound off ('three four')
Sound off ('one two ... three four')"

Before every meal we had to do five chin-ups on a metal cross bar. We learned how to low crawl quickly under strands of barbed wired while cradling our M-16 rifles in our arms. We had to run twenty-five yards carrying another soldier on our back. It took about four weeks before I got my body into good physical condition. On the day we took our final PT Test, I maxed out in four of the five events. I easily passed the fifth event, the mile run, with a time of six minutes ten seconds. Six minutes was the "max number", so I just missed being one of the few guys to max out the entire test. I was happy with the test results and that my overall physical conditioning was excellent. But the minute I completed our PT Test, I asked a buddy for a cigarette and restarted my six-year smoking habit. In 1969, a majority of the guys in our unit smoked. In Vietnam, the Army even provided free cigarettes to the field soldiers brought in by our re-supply helicopters.

Most of Fort Ord was on quarantine during my eight weeks of basic training because of a contagious meningitis outbreak. One person in my basic training company died from this disease. In order to contain the disease as much as possible, those in my unit were allowed to leave our company area only as a supervised group—no weekends off. As a result, we got to know people in our company well. I became good friends with Roger Brown. Roger was married and from Southern Utah—Mormon country. He was considered a "Jack Mormon," meaning someone who grew up in the religion but was not practicing it. Roger, "Utah" as everyone called him, was a high school dropout, a very good guitar player, happily married, and a good athlete (he maxed out the PT test) who became my closest friend over the next seventeen months. We would go through sixteen weeks of training together, fly together to Vietnam, and then were part of the same infantry unit in Vietnam.

Sgt. Perry was the Drill Sergeant for our eight weeks of basic training. He was the prototypical person for this job—smartly attired in his heavily-starched green fatigues adorned with numerous medals including the highly respected Vietnam Combat Infantry Badge, a ubiquitous and imposing brown campaign hat, and boots spit-shined to a highly reflective surface. He looked like Lou Gossett from the 1980s movie, "*An Officer and a Gentleman."* He was young, with ramrod-straight posture, an athletic build, supremely confident in his attitude, and intimidating in both his appearance and speech. He didn't talk with us; he screamed at us in his own well-refined military cadence. His speech was not only loud but creatively vulgar. He even was adept at putting swear words between syllables, such as, "I want to see every swinging Richard standing outside in "for-fxxxxing-mation" at 0500 hours." I thought I'd better be careful around this guy; he's got this military stuff down. This is not his first rodeo.

Most of the other drill sergeants I encountered were like Sgt. Perry—tough talking, physically strong, constantly in your face, and also not highly educated. I'm reasonably certain that Sgt. Perry dropped out of high school to enlist in the Army. I was surprised one evening when one of our instructors told me to report to Sgt. Perry's office immediately. This can't be good I thought to myself as I entered his office and stood at attention. "Sit down, Private Givens," he ordered in an ordinary, almost friendly tone of voice that I had never before heard. He proceeded to explain to me that he was in some financial difficulty. He was behind in his payments to one of his charge accounts and the store was demanding full and immediate payment of the entire bill. He asked me if I could write some sort of letter asking the creditor for more time to pay the bill. He had not the slightest idea how to create such a letter. It took me less than an hour to write the document for him. He seemed pleased with the wording, thanked me for writing the letter, and sent me on my way. I never heard anything more from him about this event. In fact, at our next morning formation he was nose to nose with me yelling in my face as if nothing had happened the night before. I was not surprised. Basic training was meant to toughen us up for combat, not for weak scholarly or social activities. Point made.

After eight weeks of getting myself into good physical condition, I graduated from Basic Training. I would be staying at Fort Ord for eight weeks of Advanced Infantry Training, meaning I likely would end up in Vietnam in the infantry. I desperately wanted Connie to join me in California so I could see her on the weekends. She could *not live on base, so she would have to live with a friend in San Francisco.*

Advanced Infantry Training (AIT)

After we completed eight weeks of basic training, most guys in our company continued at Fort Ord with eight more weeks of Advanced Infantry Training (AIT.) The meningitis epidemic had subsided and, on most weekends, we were given a two-day pass. Connie decided to move to San Francisco and live with Carol Thompson, a college friend and one of her bridesmaids, who was working as a United Airlines flight attendant. The drive to Ft. Ord was about two hours. I was able to leave the base on most weekends, so Connie and I spent time exploring San Francisco and the Monterey Peninsula. Several weekends we stayed at the Motel Six in Monterrey which was plenty upscale for both of us. Motel Six got its name because for many years after it was established, the room rate was six dollars per night—affordable even on my meager ninety-nine dollars per month Army salary. We loved spending time on the beautiful Monterey coast and particularly in Carmel. It was almost assured that I would be shipped out to Vietnam at the conclusion of my AIT training, so we wanted to be together as much as we could before that day.

AIT was exactly as advertised—more advanced and more intense. We learned how to fire different weapons and how to care for them. We usually went to the firing range five days a week. By 1969 the Army had switched to the M-16 automatic rifle capable of firing a full magazine (thirty rounds) in less than five seconds. We also learned to fire other small arms weapons like the M-60 machine gun, capable of firing over five-hundred rounds a minute, and the M-79 grenade launcher that can fire 40mm fragmentation grenades a distance of over three-hundred yards. Almost every night, after cleaning the barracks and spit-shining our boots, we had to break down our rifles and thoroughly clean them.

One of the most dreaded activities of our infantry training was our time in the tear gas chamber. No one looked forward to removing his gas mask after we entered a large room filled with tear gas. It seemed longer than one to two minutes before we emerged with burning, watery eyes and coughing and choking while trying to get some fresh air into our lungs.

My bunk mate for the eight weeks of AIT was Emmanuel Yonan. Yo, as we called him, had a Ph.D. in chemistry from the University of Illinois, was married, and his wife was expecting their first child. Talk about a waste of talent. Just imagine ... Dr. Yonan, a highly- educated chemist, was drafted into the military and, after sixteen weeks of training, was given the job classification of infantry (ignominiously referred to as a grunt.) When we got to Vietnam, Yo was assigned to an infantry unit like the rest of us. Yo was resourceful enough his first full day in country to locate a local Army unit analyzing Vietnam's environmental and medical diseases. He interviewed with the commanding officer and received a transfer to this unit and, to the best of my knowledge, never spent a day in the field. It's unfortunate he had to find this work on his own without any help from the Army.

During the fifth week of AIT, our first sergeant announced that all passes for the upcoming weekend were rescinded. Our entire company was to undergo an Inspector General (IG) full- dress inspection. We would have all our belongings properly displayed, boots spit shined, and bunks meticulously made to the highest Army standards. During the inspection on Saturday afternoon, we would stand at attention next to our bunks while the general slowly inspected our barracks, equipment, and every soldier in our company.

The problem with this particular IG inspection was that Connie and I had made plans to spend the weekend in Napa with our friends Gary and Jill Gregory. I thought about the consequences and decided I was going to take off to spend the weekend with Connie—essentially go AWOL (Absent Without Leave) for two days. After all, what were they going to do ... send me to Vietnam? I told my friend and bunkmate Emmanuel Yonan my plan to leave Friday night and return on Sunday evening. Yo told me, "I'll do my best to cover for you." That assurance was good enough for me.

Connie picked me up Friday evening and off we went to spend a great weekend in Napa with our friends. I never told Connie or our friends that

I was AWOL for the weekend. During our return, I asked Connie to drive the last twenty miles to Fort Ord. After we switched drivers, Connie saw me changing from my civvies (civilian clothes) to my Army greens, and asked me what was going on. I explained the situation to her and told her she needed to let me off just outside the gate and I would walk in. No surprise—she was terribly worried about what would happen to me when I returned to the company area. What kind of punishment would I be subjected to? Would she even be able to see me the next two weeks?

"Hey, Yo," I said as I approached his bunk. Everything in our barracks seemed normal and calm. In a quiet voice I asked him, "Am I in big trouble? What happened with the inspection?" Yo smiled and said, "The general came through yesterday afternoon. Everyone was on their best military behavior. The general stopped at our bunk, looked at me and asked, 'Where is Private Givens?' Sir, I snapped in my best military cadence, Private Givens is having marital problems and is with the chaplain, sir. The explanation offered was accepted without any comment and the general moved on." "Yo," I said, "You truly are a genius. I owe you one my friend."

Another of my friends during AIT was Girard Liberty, married and a graduate from Oregon State University. He is someone with whom I shared many common interests. We both had read the recently published book called *Beat the Dealer.* The book was written by a mathematics professor who determined by computer analysis (unusual technology in the 1960s) the best way to play the card game blackjack in order to win against the dealer. Every possible situation was covered in this book including when to take a card or not, what to bet, and how to calculate the ratio between high cards (tens and face cards) and other cards in a single deck. During any down time in our training, Girard and I always had a deck of cards and we practiced counting cards and playing the "blackjack system." Over many hours of practice, I learned how to count the cards accurately and when to make large bets (when the deck was above a certain ratio of tens) and when to make smaller bets. There was never any guesswork as to when to take an extra card and when to stand pat. The system tells the knowledgeable player what to do in every situation.

Later when Connie and I went to Las Vegas before I shipped out to

Vietnam, I played blackjack in several casinos and almost always walked away a winner. One club actually asked me to leave; I was winning maybe sixty dollars, and they detected I was counting cards—not illegal but frowned upon by the casino operators. Later, when I first arrived in Vietnam and before we headed out to the field, my blackjack expertise helped me send home some money. I had only sixty dollars when the poker game started during my first full day in Vietnam. By the time the deck got around to me, I was down to about twenty dollars. Dealer called the games and I said, "Let's play blackjack." In blackjack the dealer always has a huge advantage of at least 15 percent over the average player. Why? Because the player had to make a decision on whether or not to take a card before the dealer and would often bust (go over twenty-one and lose.) By the end of my three days in training, and before heading out to the field, I was able to send Connie around one-hundred-fifty dollars from my winnings (and still keep my sixty dollars.) That was big money. I only was making ninety-nine dollars a month plus a little extra for combat pay.

Unlike basic training, AIT afforded us a little free time. I had not attended church since I was seventeen, but several evenings I walked to the Episcopal Church on base. There was a certain familiarity from childhood with the liturgy of the church that gave me some comfort, even though I considered myself to be an agnostic—too smart to believe all this religious stuff. Still, I enjoyed singing in the small church choir and the respite it offered me from the daily military grind.

One of my training mates began asking me questions about my religious background. I explained I had attended church all my life through high school, but stopped any church involvement once I got to college. I told him I thought religion was a crutch many people needed, but I was not one of them. As it turns out, this was my first encounter with a practicing Mormon. He said I should read the Book of Mormon as it would help me find my faith. To the best of my recollection, I never said yes—but ... I also didn't give him an emphatic no. Several days later this new acquaintance brought me the Book of Mormon. He had walked several miles to the Mormon Chapel on post and picked up a copy for me. I had the good sense to thank him for his effort but told him most firmly I had no interest. Mormons, I found out, are prevalent throughout the Western US and they can be extraordinarily persistent. Lesson learned.

Trying to Avoid the Infantry

Vietnam was pretty much the inevitable destination for any draftee, and most draftees were given the job classification (MOS) of 11B—infantry. A person who enlists must sign up for a minimum of three years, and the Army is usually willing to spend time and money training these soldiers for specialized, non-combat jobs. A draftee only had to spend twenty-four months in the service; the Army did not normally want to give special training for such a short-term soldier. So, anyone drafted in the late 1960s was almost assuredly going to Vietnam as a grunt (a combat infantry soldier.)

I used every bit of ingenuity I could muster to try to avoid at least the infantry, if not Vietnam altogether. My test scores were high on the military intelligence test (pretty easy compared to the ACT or other college standardized tests), so with my Master's Degree and plenty of assertive action I tried to maneuver myself into some sort of cushy desk job. First, I tried language school at the Army's Language Institute in Monterey. The thought of spending the next twelve months in beautiful Monterey learning a language was much more inviting to me than the thought of maneuvering through the jungles of Southeast Asia. I would spend one year learning Vietnamese and then most likely spend the next twelve months in the only country in the world speaking that language, Vietnam. Maybe the war would be over by that time. I was told I would be accepted if ... the "if" was a big one. I had to sign up for one additional year of service. The thought of twelve additional months was a non-starter for me. I turned it down. I was already twenty-four and one-half years old and wouldn't get out until I was twenty-seven. Next, I applied for a direct commission as an officer (1st Lt. as I recall.) Once again, I received an affirmative answer except ... yes, one more year. No, thanks. Two years in the Army was going to be my max, so I accepted my fate.

I was heading for the field in Vietnam with the rest of my Fort Ord buddies.

Toward the end of AIT another possible deplyment opportunity arose. At week seven, the penultimate week of our training, a rumor was making the rounds that an order had come down from the Honor Guard Command to select twenty-six men from our AIT company to serve two years in the Honor Guard in Washington D.C. No deployment to Vietnam for these soldiers! Criteria for this assignment was that a person had to stand at least 5' 10" tall and have no police record of any kind. That latter category automatically knocked out about one-third of our company. The rumor was confirmed by our first sergeant later that week. We learned that twenty-six men would be selected by the established criteria, and the selection would be done alphabetically. I couldn't believe my good fortune. I had been working so hard on my own to avoid the infantry, and this opportunity just fell into my lap. I was a shoo-in to make the Honor Guard. I called Connie to tell her the impending good news. Not so fast soldier! This is the Army we're talking about.

At the end of the week, the list was posted with twenty-six names going all the way through to the letter "L." But, where was my name? It was not on the list. I went immediately to our records clerk and asked, "Why is my name not on the list? It should be." He examined the company roster and said, "Here's why. You reported one day late to the company" (an administrative mix-up and not really true.) "By Army regulation your name is placed at the end of the alphabet." Seriously! I was greatly disappointed with this news, but, despite my protestations to the hapless clerk and since I was beginning to understand how the military worked, I accepted my fate almost stoically. Nothin' I can do about it.

I hated the strict, over-regimented atmosphere of the Army and the little control I had over my decisions and my life. I had spent eighteen years of my life doing reasonably well in an academic setting (and becoming well-educated), but I was not using much of that accumulated knowledge in this environment. I was being trained by and taking orders from drill sergeants, most of whom were not even high school graduates and who loved to dish it out to these college boys who thought they were so smart. Nevertheless, I listened carefully to what these men were teaching; I wanted to learn all I could to help me stay alive when I went to Vietnam. And, there was little doubt that almost all the soldiers that I was training with in 1969 were headed for that country and that war. Our lives belonged to the United States Army and they needed more troops in Vietnam. We were fresh meat. I had lost not only my independence but also my personal identity. I was just a faceless number to the military and part of a large group of new recruits training for war.

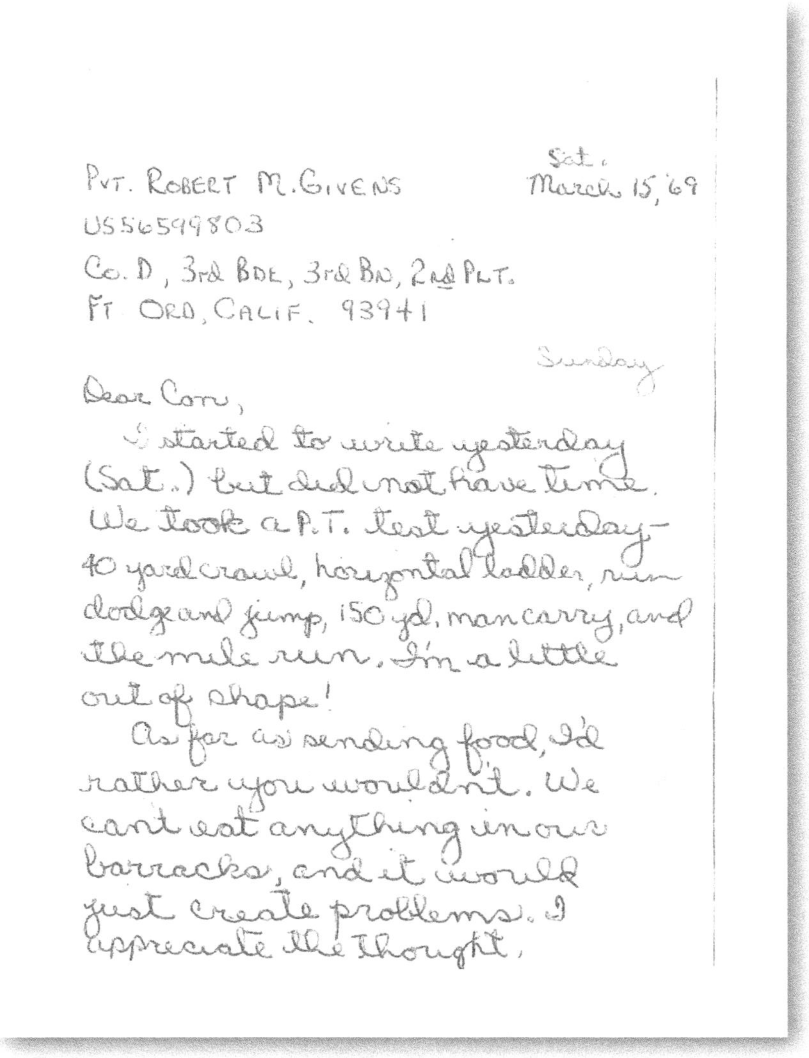

Pvt. Robert M. Givens
US56599803
Co. D, 3rd Bde, 3rd Bn, 2nd Plt.
Ft. Ord, Calif. 93941

Sat.
March 15, '69

Sunday

Dear Con,

I started to write yesterday (Sat.) but did not have time. We took a P.T. test yesterday— 40 yard crawl, horizontal ladder, run dodge and jump, 150 yd. man carry, and the mile run. I'm a little out of shape!

As far as sending food, I'd rather you wouldn't. We cant eat anything in our barracks, and it would just create problems. I appreciate the thought.

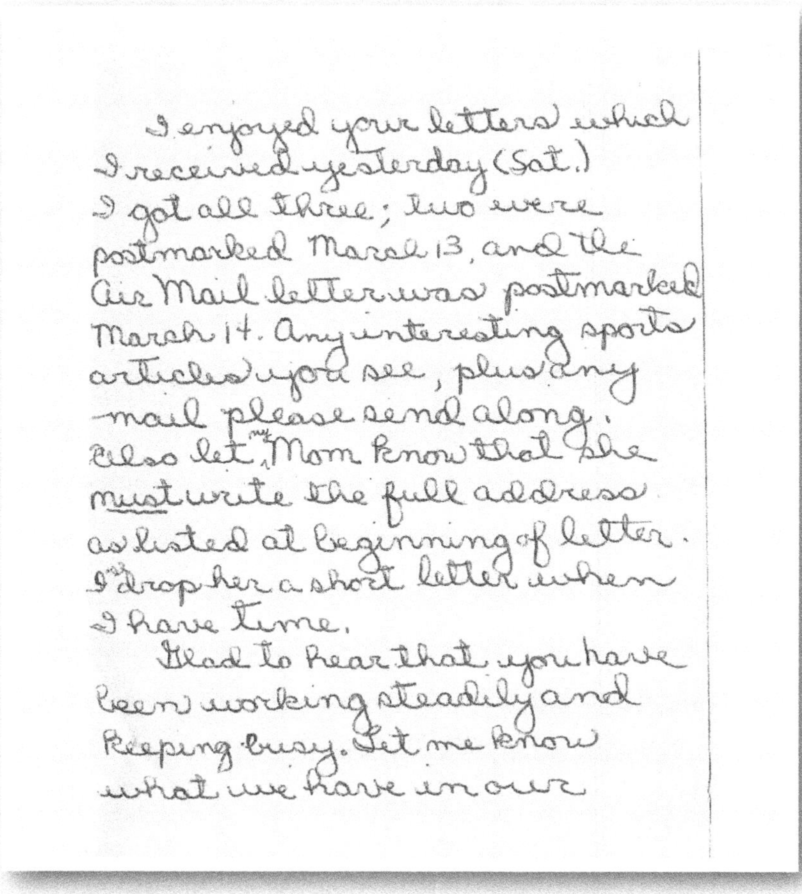

I enjoyed your letters which I received yesterday (Sat.) I got all three; two were postmarked March 13, and the Air Mail letter was postmarked March 14. Any interesting sports articles you see, plus any mail please send along. Also let my Mom know that she must write the full address as listed at beginning of letter. I'll drop her a short letter when I have time.

Glad to hear that you have been working steadily and keeping busy. Let me know what we have in our

(3)

savings and checking acc't.

Tues., March 18

Sunday I had K.P. from 7:00 A.M. until 6:30 P.M., so I couldn't finish the letter or call. The phones are in one room, which our platoon can only use on certain occasions. Sunday our platoon was in that room from 8:15 A.M to 9:30 A.M, but I couldn't call. Needless to say, I had K.P. on the worst possible day; our only day off.

I got the three letters today (one was postmarked Air Mail from Davenport, Mar. 14) It's great to hear from you

and what you're doing. Sometimes in the late afternoon, I
think that you're
getting home from school
or getting ready to eat. Boy,
I really appreciate a refrigerator
with cold pop, a pickle, etc.
Haven't had a candy bar or
beer or pop since I've been
here. Also since you're 2 hours
ahead, we're starting our
afternoon exercises (1:00 P.M)
when you're about ready
to leave school (3:00 P.M.)

Some of the classes are
fairly interesting like first
aid, and hand to hand
combat. Others are very
boring and stupid. There

(5)

is a lot of propaganda around about Win in Vietnam or "Charley" (the enemy). Of course the Army is the infantry and the infantry is the Vietnam War right now.

I don't think I'll have time to write any [redacted] letters to friends, but send letters we get on. I'll be interested to see what happens to Doug. I may cash that check I brought. If I do I will let you know the amount. Also I took the marriage certificate to the 1st Sergeant tonight

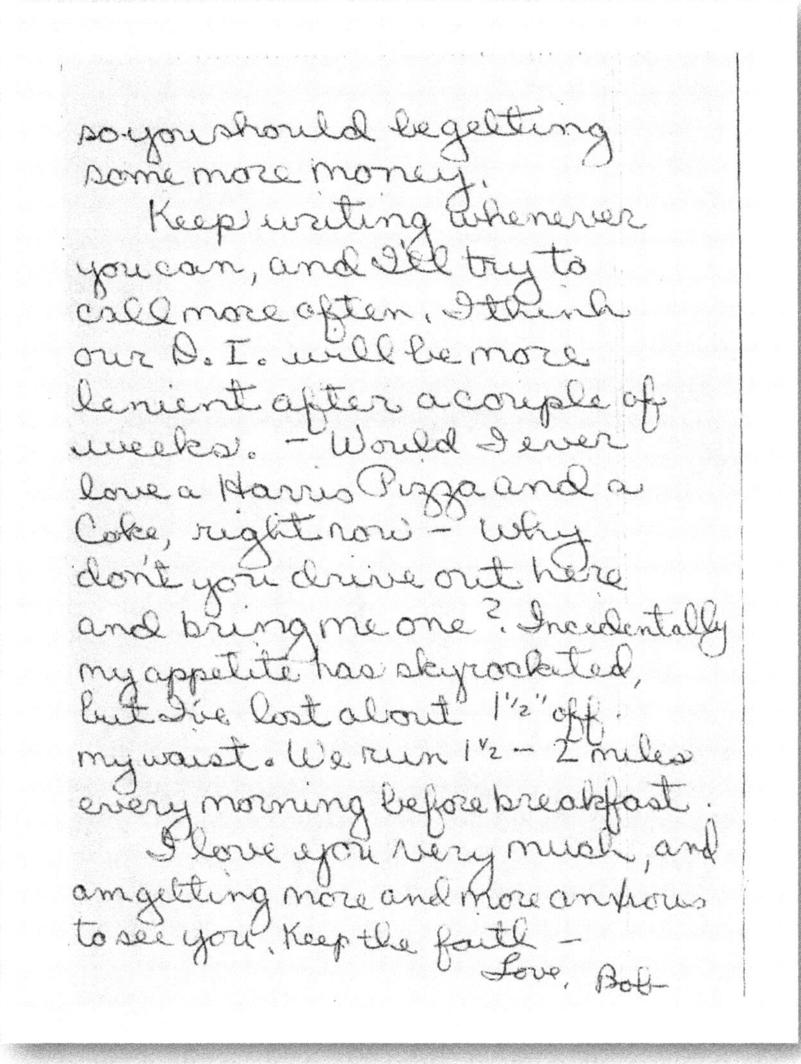

so you should be getting
some more money.
Keep writing whenever
you can, and I'll try to
call more often. I think
our D. I. will be more
lenient after a couple of
weeks. - Would I ever
love a Harris Pizza and a
Coke, right now - Why
don't you drive out here
and bring me one? Incidentally
my appetite has skyrocketed,
but I've lost about 1½" off
my waist. We run 1½ - 2 miles
every morning before breakfast.
I love you very much, and
am getting more and more anxious
to see you. Keep the faith -
Love, Bob

April 30, 1969

Hi Hon,

A little more time to write tonight. We are done with our training!! Spent most of today cleaning our gear to turn in tomorrow. After graduation we have a seven hour pass on Friday, from 3:00 to 10:00. Pete Gardelos, myself, and 3 or 4 other guys plan to go to Monterey and have a good steak dinner. Then Sat. afternoon we will move out of our B.C.T. barracks and into new residence – don't know where, but someplace on base.

Your husband is much more physically fit than 8 weeks ago. We took our final P.T. test last Thursday and I scored

441 pts. out of a possible 500. The first test we took I scored 275. I ran the mile in 7:00 (Thursday) as opposed to 10:20 on my first try 7 weeks ago. So, physically I feel pretty good, and have lost about 2 or 3 inches around waist and 15 - 20 pounds.

The best news today is that I was promoted to E-2. I now have one little stripe on my jacket and will be making $15 more a month (rolling in dough....) Got paid today - $43. You should be receiving $100 fairly soon.

As I mentioned in my last letter, Charles is not in any trouble. Mom lost her job, apparently because the bill collectors were hounding her at work. She called Charles and asked him what he was going to do about it. He said there wasn't much else he could do but have her go down there to live with them. He is driving to Decatur sometime to take Mom down to Nashville. A rather confused — but typical — situation.

I dont have any more information concerning my M.O.S. or future status. I was assuming that after basic I would either go to a school (e.g.) language) or O.J.T. (similar to Dale). In either of these cases you would probably be able to come with me. However, it appears that I may be going to an A.I.T. school in which I would be required to live in

army barracks. Still, I'm only
speculating at this point, and
the only thing I can say is
to be prepared for anything.
I will call when possible –
I love you very much and wish
the time would go faster.

Love,
Bob

P.S.
Sending a letter I got from my Cousin
Michele –
remember
Reno?

My home on South Westlawn Ave. in Decatur, Illinois where I lived until age eleven. Our neighbors were doctors, lawyers and business executives. Between age eleven and twenty we moved to eight different rental properties

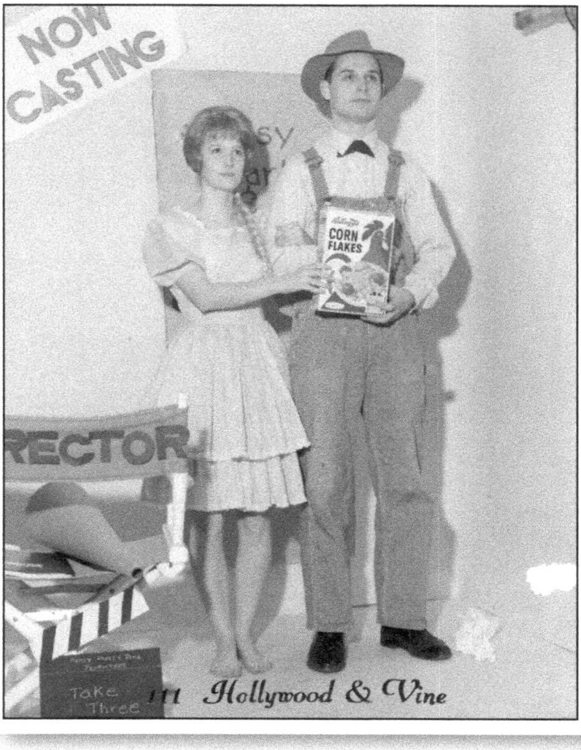

Connie and I began dating in 1965 during my junior year at Millikin University in Decatur. This picture is from one of the dances at our fraternity house.

My picture from college in 1965. I was a Biology major and an active member of SAE fraternity, president of the Interfraternity Council, and president of the senior class.

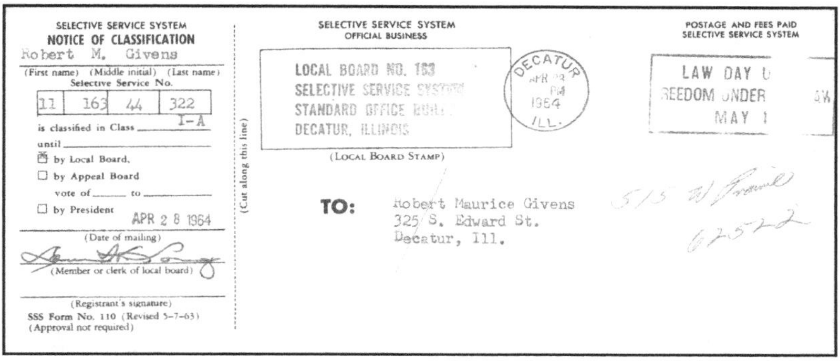

SELECTIVE SERVICE SYSTEM
NOTICE OF CLASSIFICATION
Robert M. Givens
(First name) (Middle initial) (Last name)
Selective Service No.
11 | 163 | 44 | 322
is classified in Class I-A
until
☒ by Local Board,
☐ by Appeal Board
vote of ____ to ____
☐ by President
APR 2 8 1964
(Date of mailing)
(Member or clerk of local board)
(Registrant's signature)
SSS Form No. 110 (Revised 5-7-63)
(Approval not required)

(Cut along this line)

SELECTIVE SERVICE SYSTEM
OFFICIAL BUSINESS

LOCAL BOARD NO. 163
SELECTIVE SERVICE SYSTEM
STANDARD OFFICE BUIL
DECATUR, ILLINOIS
(LOCAL BOARD STAMP)

DECATUR
APR 28
PM
1964
ILL.

POSTAGE AND FEES PAID
SELECTIVE SERVICE SYSTEM

LAW DAY U
REEDOM UNDER
MAY 1

TO: Robert Maurice Givens
325 S. Edward St.
Decatur, Ill.

515 W Prairie
62522

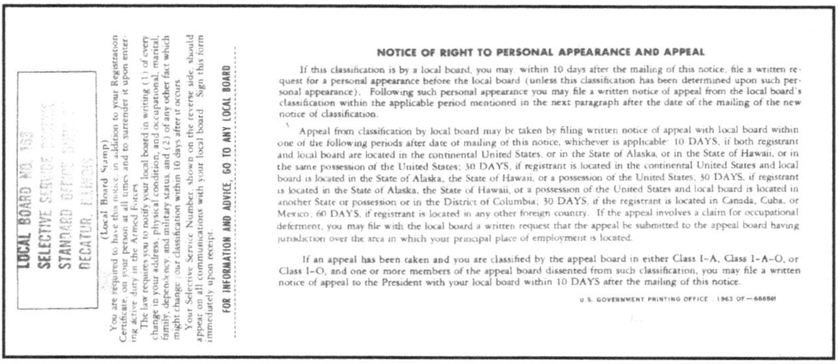

LOCAL BOARD NO. 163
SELECTIVE SERVICE SYSTEM
STANDARD OFFICE BUIL
DECATUR, ILLINOIS
(Local Board Stamp)

You are required to have this notice, in addition to your Registration Certificate, on your person at all times and to surrender it upon entering active duty in the Armed Forces.

The law requires you to notify your local board in writing (1) of every change in your address, physical condition, and occupational, marital, family, dependency, and military status, and (2) of any other fact which might change your classification within 10 days after it occurs.

Your Selective Service Number, shown on the reverse side, should appear on all communications with your local board. Sign this form immediately upon receipt.

FOR INFORMATION AND ADVICE, GO TO ANY LOCAL BOARD

NOTICE OF RIGHT TO PERSONAL APPEARANCE AND APPEAL

If this classification is by a local board, you may, within 10 days after the mailing of this notice, file a written request for a personal appearance before the local board (unless this classification has been determined upon such personal appearance). Following such personal appearance you may file a written notice of appeal from the local board's classification within the applicable period mentioned in the next paragraph after the date of the mailing of the new notice of classification.

Appeal from classification by local board may be taken by filing written notice of appeal with local board within one of the following periods after date of mailing of this notice, whichever is applicable: 10 DAYS, if both registrant and local board are located in the continental United States, or in the State of Alaska, or in the State of Hawaii, or in the same possession of the United States; 30 DAYS, if registrant is located in the continental United States and local board is located in the State of Alaska, the State of Hawaii, or a possession of the United States; 30 DAYS, if registrant is located in the State of Alaska, the State of Hawaii, or a possession of the United States and local board is located in another State or possession or in the District of Columbia; 30 DAYS, if the registrant is located in Canada, Cuba, or Mexico; 60 DAYS, if registrant is located in any other foreign country. If the appeal involves a claim for occupational deferment, you may file with the local board a written request that the appeal be submitted to the appeal board having jurisdiction over the area in which your principal place of employment is located.

If an appeal has been taken and you are classified by the appeal board in either Class I-A, Class I-A-O, or Class I-O, and one or more members of the appeal board dissented from such classification, you may file a written notice of appeal to the President with your local board within 10 DAYS after the mailing of this notice.

U.S. GOVERNMENT PRINTING OFFICE : 1963 OF—686801

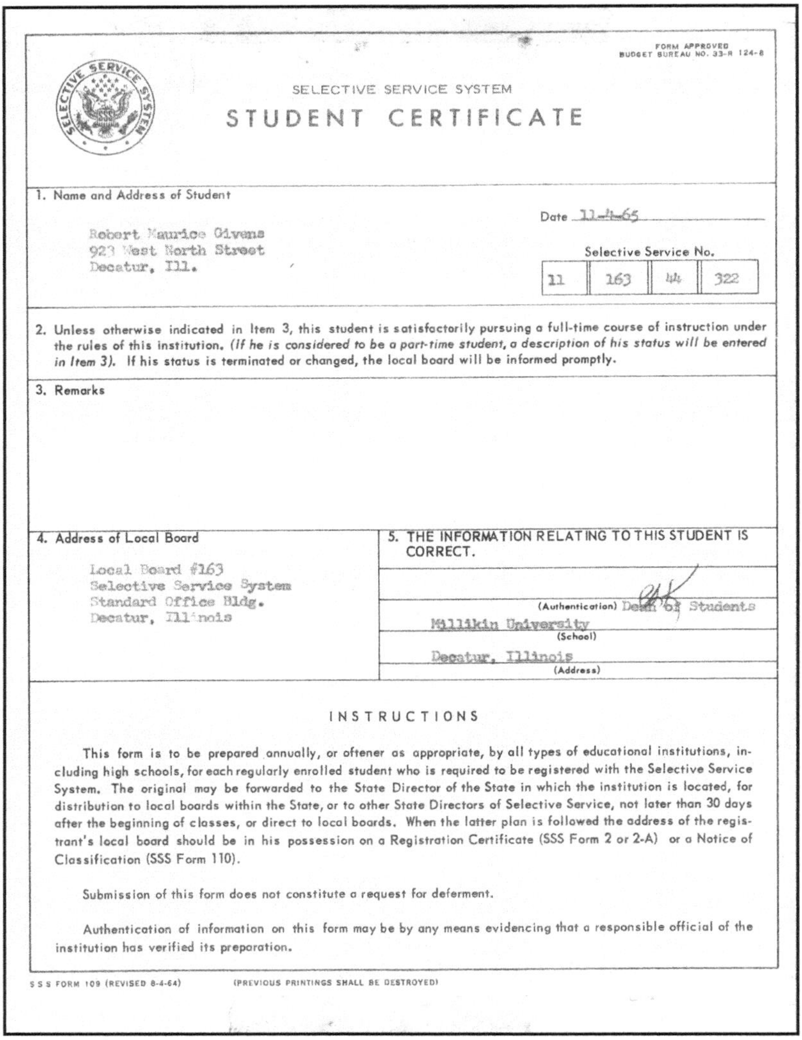

FORM APPROVED
BUDGET BUREAU NO. 33-R 124-8

SELECTIVE SERVICE SYSTEM

STUDENT CERTIFICATE

1. Name and Address of Student

Robert Maurice Givens
923 West North Street
Decatur, Ill.

Date 11-4-65

Selective Service No.

11	163	44	322

2. Unless otherwise indicated in Item 3, this student is satisfactorily pursuing a full-time course of instruction under the rules of this institution. *(If he is considered to be a part-time student, a description of his status will be entered in Item 3).* If his status is terminated or changed, the local board will be informed promptly.

3. Remarks

4. Address of Local Board

Local Board #163
Selective Service System
Standard Office Bldg.
Decatur, Illinois

5. THE INFORMATION RELATING TO THIS STUDENT IS CORRECT.

(Authentication) Dean of Students

Millikin University
(School)

Decatur, Illinois
(Address)

INSTRUCTIONS

This form is to be prepared annually, or oftener as appropriate, by all types of educational institutions, including high schools, for each regularly enrolled student who is required to be registered with the Selective Service System. The original may be forwarded to the State Director of the State in which the institution is located, for distribution to local boards within the State, or to other State Directors of Selective Service, not later than 30 days after the beginning of classes, or direct to local boards. When the latter plan is followed the address of the registrant's local board should be in his possession on a Registration Certificate (SSS Form 2 or 2-A) or a Notice of Classification (SSS Form 110).

Submission of this form does not constitute a request for deferment.

Authentication of information on this form may be by any means evidencing that a responsible official of the institution has verified its preparation.

SSS FORM 109 (REVISED 8-4-64) (PREVIOUS PRINTINGS SHALL BE DESTROYED)

The selective service classification and student certificate were important documents for men eighteen to twenty-five. I was listed as I-A but the draft board had made an error and changed it to a student deferment.

Mr. and Mrs. Glen A. Richeson
request the honour of your presence
at the marriage of their daughter
Connie
to
Mr. Robert M. Givens
on Saturday, the nineteenth of August
Nineteen hundred and sixty-seven
at four o'clock
South Park Presbyterian Church
Rock Island, Illinois

Our wedding announcement which Connie's parents sent out to over 200 guests. We were engaged over Christmas in 1966 and married the next August in her hometown of Rock Island, Illinois.

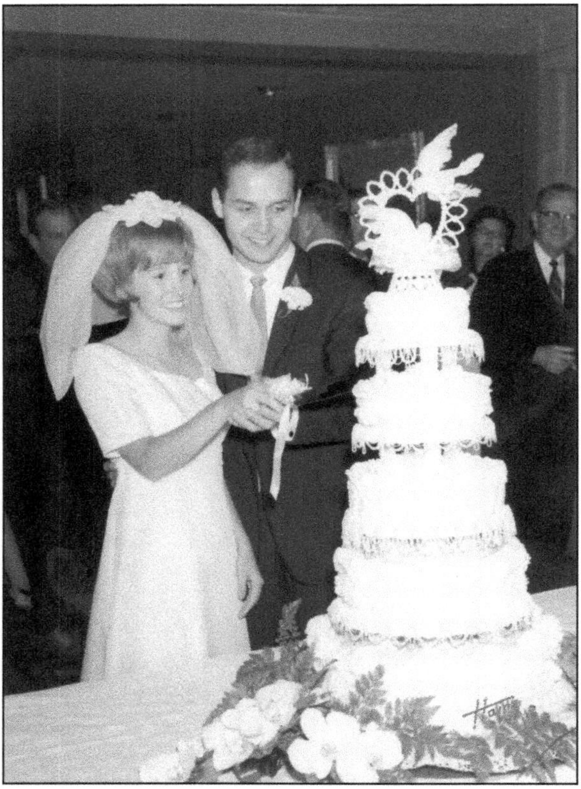

Connie and I are cutting the decorative five-layer wedding cake during the celebration dinner. I was glad that neither my Mom nor I had to pay for the expensive dinner.

Connie's bridesmaids and her mother before the wedding. Twelve-year old Lynette Richeson, was a bridesmaid for her big sister as was Carol Thompson on the left. Connie lived with Carol in San Francisco during my Army training.

The first year of our married life I was an Assistant Head Counselor in Wright Quadrangle at Indiana University, an all-men's residence hall with 1000 men. Connie was one of only three women living there.

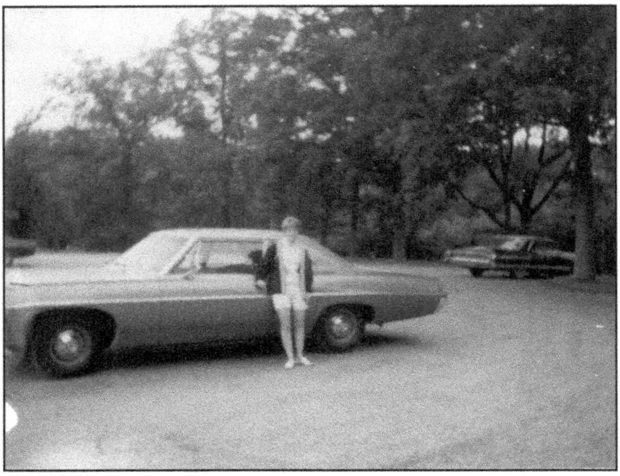

Homer, our first car, was a barebones, cheapest model Chevy with a small six-cylinder engine, no power options and not even a radio. I put Connie's engraved seat belt in the middle of the front seat so she would always sit next to me.

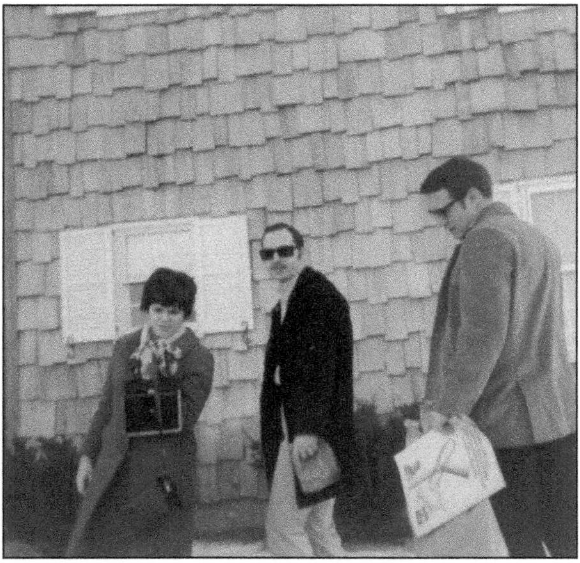

Our first real home was a furnished one-bedroom apartment in Willimantic, Connecticut. Our friends, Doug and Meg Keller visited us on several occasions and we traveled around New England, including into Boston.

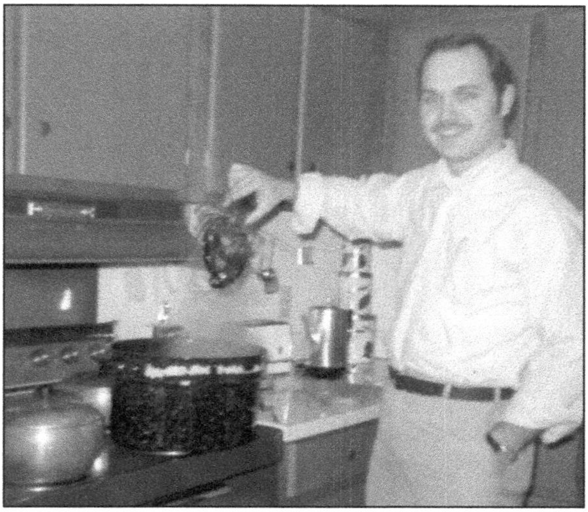

Our first time in New England and we bought live lobsters on the Connecticut coast and brought them home to be cooked. The lobsters were not particularly happy about that.

I was drafted in February 1969. Everyone drafted that year was headed to the war in Vietnam.

Two friends Emanuel Yonan and Girard Liberty who were part of my Advanced Infantry Training at Fort Ord, California. Both went on to serve in Vietnam.

After training and before leaving for Vietnam, Connie and I were able to travel around California and see sites like the Hearst Castle, in San Simeon. Notice the military haircut.

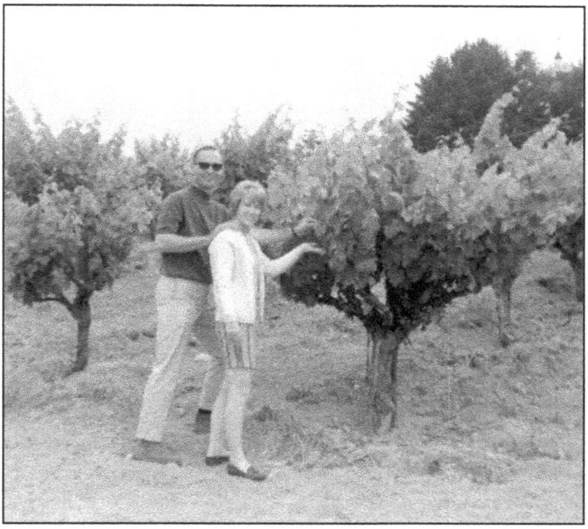

Connie and I spent time with friends in Napa, California and took a tour of the wine country.

We were living it up in Las Vegas staying at Howard Hughes' fancy Landmark Hotel, a giant step above our normal place (Motel Six). This was my first opportunity to test the blackjack system and I won enough to cover the cost of the room.

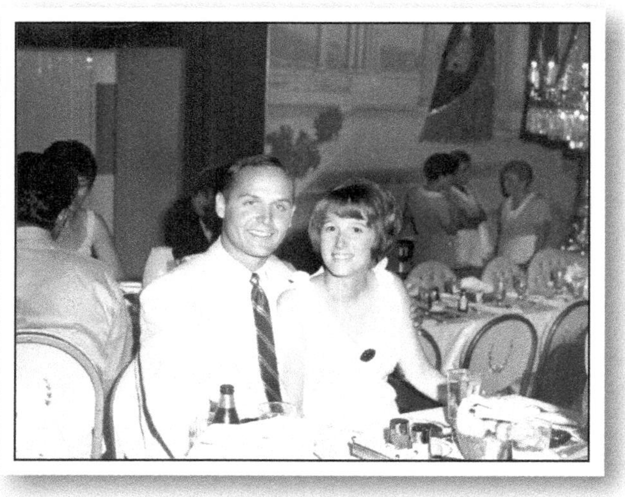

Connie and I are enjoying a fancy dinner at one of several shows we attended in we Las Vegas. We spent a week in Las Vegas and Reno before I left for Vietnam.

— FOUR —

Off to War

Preparing to leave Country

My orders were to report to Travis Air Force Base on July 21, 1969, for deployment to the Republic of South Vietnam. US Army tours in Vietnam were for twelve months—three-hundred-sixty-five days. And, for sure, we were all counting. I received orders for Vietnam and my Military Occupational Specialty (MOS) during the last week of training at Fort Ord. Not surprisingly, my MOS was 11B ... infantry. Yes, I know, did I really expect the Army to make use of a person with degrees in biology and higher education and experience working in student personnel at a major college? Unlikely, at best. I was assigned to the infantry like most every other draftee at the time.

Connie and I had known for some months that this day was coming but we just tried to focus on each other. During the three weeks from the end of training to my deployment to Vietnam, we spent every minute of every day together. Our conversations did not dwell on the negatives of our upcoming separation. We discussed some timely and some mundane topics, like the importance of frequent letters between us, the possibility of a mid-tour R&R the Army provided, and Connie's new job teaching fifth grade. We enjoyed ourselves and laughed a lot during these weeks away from Army interference. As much as possible prior to my leaving, we tried to be like a normal couple on vacation. As we drove long distances through California and Nevada, Connie tested me on various blackjack scenarios and what I should do in certain situations according to the blackjack book. Connie never liked to gamble. She thought it was simply putting your money into someone else's piggy bank. However, if I was going to try playing blackjack with our money, she thought "I may as well try to help him win."

We toured some of the national parks in California, we visited sites in and around San Francisco, we spent time in Las Vegas, and we traveled to Reno where we saw my relatives and I played some blackjack (and won a little money.) We knew our time was short but we made the best of it and even created some lasting memories. When we left Las Vegas to drive to Reno, I asked the Vegas gas station attendant how to get to Reno (no GPS in 1969.) Gas stations in those days had working attendants who not only pumped gas, checked oil, and washed windshields, they also gave directions. His words were for us to "take a right out of the gas station, proceed east for three stoplights, turn left and go four-hundred-fifty miles!" He was right. Not a stop light or a stop sign in all those miles, only rocks and desert.

My deployment was delayed by one day for reasons unknown to me (there would be a lot of that "unknown reasoning" in the Army). So, Connie and I were able to return to San Francisco for one last day before I flew out the evening of July 22. As a result, I was able to watch the Apollo 11 Spacecraft landing and Neil Armstrong becoming the first person to walk on the moon, thus fulfilling President Kennedy's inaugural-speech goal to "land a person on the moon in this decade."

On July 22, I boarded a Seaboard World Airlines 707 commercial jet at Travis Air Force Base located between San Francisco and Sacramento, California, headed for Vietnam. I was told there were some war protesters surrounding the base, but I do not remember seeing any of them. I was paying full attention to my wife as we held each other closely and repeatedly hugged, kissed, and then, through tear-streaked eyes, said goodbye. This moment of leaving Connie was incredibly difficult. Even though we had months to get ready for this day, the separation was terribly painful because there was no way for us to know how this saga would end. The daily death count of Americans was apparent to everyone who watched the news or read the papers. Connie and I never dared talk about or even openly considered some kind of horrible ending to this tour of duty, but, of course, we knew the unthinkable possibilities. And one year—fifty-two weeks—seemed like an eternity. If there was a plausible alternative to getting on this plane, I might have taken it. Leaving my wife to go and face unknown dangers for the next twelve months was the last thing in the world I wanted to do. We both realized we would not see each other for a very long time. The most we had been separated in almost two years of marriage was for two days. I turned and sadly waved goodbye to Connie, trying my best to appear strong and confident. She drove away with her parents who had come to California to take her back to Illinois. Her childhood residence in Rock Island, Illinois, would be her home for the next twelve months. Although we never spoke the words, neither of us were sure at this moment that we would ever see each other again.

There were around one-hundred-eighty soldiers on that flight headed to Bien Hoa Air Base about fifty miles from Saigon. The mood on the plane was unexpectedly upbeat—friendly and rather carefree. At times there was some bravado guy talk and laughter. Very few showed any signs of worry or concern. We were young, strong, and reasonably well-trained. We did not want to think more deeply or darkly beyond this night on the plane. We were heading into war, but you wouldn't have known it until much later.

My friend, Utah, got out his guitar and started a portion of the plane singing 1960s folk songs. Utah was genuine, unassuming, and honest—all traits I respected. He wasn't a worrier and just took things as they came; his attitude helped me do the same. Although his formal education ended after about 10th grade, I found Utah was plenty savvy. Over time I learned from Utah, and other soldiers during my tour in Vietnam, that formal education had little to do with practical intelligence. Knowing proper grammar and reading classic books were much less important in this environment than maintaining your rifle and watching your buddy's back. Those lessons were important ones for me—someone who initially thought his education somehow made him a bit superior to anyone else in the company. We refueled and deplaned briefly in Hawaii.

During the flight, I pulled out my official US Army Records folder that each soldier hand-carried to Vietnam. I was hopeful that my academic background and high scores on the Army intelligence tests would help me land a coveted "rear area" job. I smiled when I noticed the results of my Army typing test. I couldn't type; I never took a typing class in my life; I wondered, why did I even take that stupid test? The record showed that I "passed" my Army typing test with 18 words per minute (15 wpm was passing.) That number was hand written on my record in black pen. I thought, hmm, you never know. Maybe that typing "skill" could help me some day. So, I embellished my score by manually changing the "18 wpm" to "48 wpm."

The announcement that changed our tone on the plane was that we soon would be landing in Vietnam. Instructions were given on deplaning, including bunker locations near the tarmac in case of incoming artillery fire. Those instructions were an abrupt wake-up call. OK, we obviously were not landing in Honolulu International Airport or anything resembling that city. Our mood was no longer casual and nonchalant; we were suddenly observant and wary.

Utah and I spent three days at an orientation program in Bien Hoa where we received instructions from soldiers who had recently been in the field. We were particularly warned about mines and sappers in the I Corps area of the country, the Northern-most area of South Vietnam where most of us were headed. Sappers were North Vietnamese soldiers (Viet Cong) who infiltrated US forces in the field or at small US landing zone encampments to set up deadly booby traps or to try to kill unexpecting troops. We were told the I Corps area of Vietnam was ripe with these sappers, presumably because so many Viet Cong (VC) troops could carry out destructive activities and then flee north across the Demilitarized Zone (DMZ.) Mines were more prevalent in this area of the country than anywhere else—from grenades strung with almost invisible, thin wires across walking paths to Bouncing Betty pressure plate bombs buried under dirt roads. The large pressure plate devices were powerful enough to knock out a tank. After three days in classes we learned we were assigned to the Americal Division's 198th Infantry Brigade, 5th of 46th Infantry Division and would be joining our infantry company the next afternoon.

My first letter from Vietnam. I wanted Connie to know I

had arrived safely and that I felt relatively safe at this fairly large Army base. I was even learning some Vietnamese words (while on KP duty!). The AWOL cartoon on page one was particularly appropriate given my experience during AIT.

Going to the Field

Utah and I boarded our first Army helicopter, a "Huey," that was used to transport troops and supplies. All of our gear for living on the land for the next thirty days was loaded into our backpacks as we boarded the chopper and sat with our legs dangling over the side. The machine-gunner assigned to this helicopter was positioned on the other side. The chopper flew only about fifty feet over the tree tops, so we got a clear view of the landscape made up of fields of rice patties and flat grassy fields. As we approached the area where our company was located, we saw two bodies on the ground that appeared to be dead North Vietnamese soldiers. The chopper circled about two-hundred yards away from the bodies and landed in a field where our company had set up a circular perimeter. First Sergeant Williams, a forty-year-old three-tour Vietnam veteran, hustled over to us and yelled over the roaring sound of the whirling helicopter blades, "Givens, Brown, glad to see you both. You are assigned to Bravo Platoon with Leslie Van Bieber, your platoon sergeant. Check in with him. You both will be combat veterans by the end of the day. We just killed two enemy soldiers an hour ago."

An hour later we walked out in single file with our platoon to check out the dead soldiers. Wow! Two hours into my first day in the field and I'm already seeing my first military casualties. A couple of hours later, after we returned from our patrol, I would see my second. Sergeant Van Bieber showed Utah and me where to position ourselves behind a long-running ditch. He had us spread out to guard our perimeter to prevent enemy soldiers from infiltrating our position. It wasn't long before I heard the cackling sound of an AK-47 rifle fired in automatic mode, "cack-cack-cack-cack." I never before had heard that sound, but every Vietnam combat veteran remembers to this day the distinctive, ominous sound made by these Russian-made rifles. Thirty seconds later I heard one of our guys about thirty yards to my right yell, "Medic, medic!" One of our soldiers positioned at the end of our row had been shot. A Medevac helicopter was brought in for rescue as darkness was closing in. We learned that night that Talbott died before reaching the hospital. I heard from others in our company a frightening fact—Talbott was "short," meaning that he had less than sixty days to serve in country. Utah and I were more than slightly stunned by the events of this first day. We remained on guard and wide awake throughout the rest of the evening and most of the night. I said to Utah, "I don't want to be here for ten months and then get killed like Talbott. If that's going to happen, do it now and get it over with." I didn't really know what I was saying, but as night settled in I realized our training was over. We were in real-life (and death) combat.

This is my first letter from the field. I didn't want to worry Connie by telling her about one of our guys getting killed my first day. I am already beginning to question the value of our field maneuvers. We were going from village to village looking for enemy soldiers (VC) interrogating the peasant farmers. The VC pretty much knew where we were; we had to go looking for them.

Our first month in the field was spent mainly in the central plain area of I Corps with lots of fields, small villages, and plenty of water-soaked rice paddies. At night we would form a circular perimeter with our company of around seventy to eighty soldiers. Night time, particularly on moonless or cloudy nights, was the most dangerous. In this type of rural darkness, you can barely see twenty feet in front of you. We set up nighttime positions of three soldiers with one soldier always awake on a rotating basis. Particularly for the rookies, any sound or perceived movement in the darkness put the soldier on high alert and in a very tense state of mind. We didn't have night-vision goggles. About 0200 hours one night during my first two weeks in the field, I thought I saw some movement through the hazy, fog-filled darkness about fifty feet away. I squinted my eyes and peered intently toward the spot. Was that somebody moving out there? I waited a few seconds and then I thought I saw it again and I opened fire.

Immediately everyone else in the company was firing rounds. After less than a minute, one of the officers yelled, "Cease fire!" There was silence with no incoming fire. I had apparently seen nothing. The first sergeant came over and asked who fired the first shot. I said that I thought I saw somebody moving around and fired my rifle. He scowled at me and said, "You've got to shout outgoing when you fire so our troops know we're not taking incoming rounds." Then he said to this rookie rather sarcastically, "Givens, if the gooks didn't know where we were tonight, they sure as hell know now." Not an auspicious beginning for me.

The first few weeks in the field were all a learning experience for me. Everything was new. I watched where other guys walked during the day, where they kept their weapons when we took a break, how they cared for their weapons, and how they set up their positions for nighttime defense. Nights in the field were the scariest times. Bad things happened at night. The Viet Cong soldiers knew the landscape well and were adept at guerilla war tactics. Once darkness settled in, we lost one of the most important of our five basic senses—sight. From my earlier experience when I imagined I saw movement and opened fire, I knew that lack of clear sight could play tricks on my mind. We all pretty much had to depend on our hearing as we guarded our company's position each night. To keep us awake and on guard at night, Sgt. Williams would sometimes tell us that we had intel that said we might come under attack tonight, so stay alert. OK, that was not a problem for most of us.

One of the few letters to Connie where I describe the daily activities for a combat soldier, and the only letter I mention (very briefly) a fire fight where we were engaged with and firing at enemy troops in close quarters. I also was sad that none of Connie's letters had yet reached me. I had no doubt she had written; the letters just hadn't arrived.

At the end of three weeks in the field, Captain Dan Martin, our company commander, sent word around that he needed a new Radio Telephone Operator (RTO). I volunteered for a couple of reasons. I hated being on the perimeter each night and staring into the darkness with intense anticipation for any movement or sign of enemy activity. Besides the incident when I opened fire at night without yelling outgoing, I also had an accident setting up a smoke grenade. If enemy soldiers tried to overrun our nighttime perimeter, we set up a trip wire attached to a colored smoke grenade. The tripped wire would pull the pin on the grenade, send up smoke, and give us advance warning. As I was setting up the grenade, the handle of the grenade slipped and went off in my hand. My hand was burned badly enough that I couldn't hold a pen to write Connie a letter for over a week. The second reason I volunteered was because it was apparent to me that RTOs had a better chance of being selected for the two coveted rear-area jobs that existed in an infantry company—company clerk and mail clerk. I let Captain Martin know that I had a Master's degree and that may have helped me get selected for the RTO job. Captain Martin and I had something else in common; he was a graduate and former football star at the University of Vermont whose big rival was my former school, UConn.

I was thrilled to receive Connie's letters that finally arrived (twelve of them actually.) Knowing that she was thinking and caring about me was evident from her letters and was a great comfort throughout the year. I told her in this letter about volunteering to carry a radio.

New Job as RTO

I strapped the thirty-pound PRC-25 radio on my back and carried it for the next five months. It didn't take me long to learn the lingo and protocol of radio operation. Also, radio care was minimal as these devices were extremely durable. RTOs in Vietnam were forced to swap their M-16 rifles for a .45 caliber pistol and an M-79 grenade launcher. Those weapons were fine with me; I was never a good marksman with the rifle. The radio had an antenna that easily identified this soldier as the communication link for the squad and therefore a potential target for the enemy. Still, I preferred the job that allowed me to sleep inside our nighttime perimeter with the officers and first sergeant.

We returned to our base camp, LZ Gator, on August 31. I'm on bunker guard with two others, which allows me time to write when I'm not on watch. I complain that these guys all seem so young and I'm more serious-minded than they are. I am also frustrated by our field activities and how useless they seem. I asked Connie to send me books. Over the year, Connie sent me twenty-five to thirty books.

We spent the first two weeks of September at LZ Gator where I had guard duty most nights. The LZ was much safer than the field. In mid-September, we were transported to the mountainous region of northern South Vietnam. The terrain and environment were much different than in the central plains, and it was the beginning of the rainy season. Half of South Vietnam's annual rainfall came in the monsoon months of September, October and November—over eleven inches fell per month. We were walking through heavily forested areas, mostly jungles, having to climb some steep slippery slopes and traverse several fast-flowing creeks and small rivers. We encountered leeches in these waters. I had never before seen these ugly, blood-sucking worms. After wading through the water, some of the soldiers found these parasites attached to their legs and groin areas. Removing them was not easy. They had to apply heat from the tips of their lighted cigarettes to these slimy, gross-looking critters to get them to let go so they could be pulled out. This was a rare instance when cigarettes could be good for your health.

During one break in our maneuvers through Vietnam's highlands dense with trees, we stopped for a smoke break. As we settled in and took off our backpacks, suddenly, seemingly out of nowhere, I heard a couple of shots fired in our direction. A bullet struck a tree a few inches above the head of one of our guys who was leaning with his back against the base of the tree. We all hit the ground and were ready to fire, but there were no more shots. No one was hurt, but it was clear that the VC knew where we were and were tracking us.

We stayed in the mountain jungles for a couple of weeks and we had to deal with the discomforts of living and sleeping outside in these rainy conditions every day. Vietnam was normally steamy hot and humid during the days, with humidity averaging over 80% during the summer and fall months. During the rainy season, and in the mountain areas, nights could sometimes get cold enough that we needed to use our Army-issued lightweight ponchos for warmth.

The mountains and the jungles were particularly nasty in monsoon season. I provided Connie a fairly descriptive account of some of our activities in the difficult conditions. Connie was sending me boxes of goodies at least twice a month and in this letter, I gave her a grocery list. Most guys were not so fortunate.

In late September, Captain Martin relayed to me the numbers of about fifteen soldiers he was promoting from Private First Class (PFC) to Specialist 4th Class (Spec 4). Each soldier in the unit had a specific number. We never used anyone's name when transmitting, in case the enemy was listening and could use these names to their advantage. Later that day I called back to the rear area with sixteen promotions, not fifteen. I just added my number to the rather long list and promoted myself to Spec 4. No one was ever the wiser (except now—I hope Captain Martin is not reading this story.)

Life-Saving Illness

On October 3, I got very sick with flu-like symptoms. My body was shaking periodically and I was barely able to carry my radio. The symptoms persisted for two days. Doc, Ron Berquist our company medic (who was not a medical doctor or nurse but who had received Army medical training), told the commanding officer that Givens and Klaith were running temperatures over 103 degrees. Early that afternoon a helicopter landed in our midst to bring in the weekly supplies. We were never sure when these choppers would arrive, but they were always welcome sights as they brought important items like canned food (C Rations), warm soda, warm beer, cigarettes, and, most important, letters from home. Sergeant Williams hustled over and yelled, "Givens, you and Klaith get on the chopper now, you're heading back to the rear area". I asked, "Who do I give my radio to?" The sergeant said," Give it to Private Haynes."

We climbed into the chopper and headed back to our permanent company rear area location at a spot called Landing Zone Gator. LZ Gator was no more than a secured area of about twenty acres with a helicopter landing pad and a few semi-permanent buildings. There were several large wooden-floored tents with about thirty cots for sleeping quarters. We had our own small mess hall and a one-room infirmary with an army medical doctor. Infantrymen were expected to be out in the field most of the time, not in the rear area, so there was nothing glamorous about an army landing zone.

I hit the cot when we returned and slept soundly until early evening. I wasn't interested or even able to eat anything. Suddenly, I heard some voices shouting loudly and instinctively grabbed for my weapon. The voices were coming from the executive officer and our two company clerks who were monitoring our company's activity over the radio. "We're under mortar attack," the XO (Executive Officer) shouted as I joined him in the company's headquarters barracks. "It's still in progress and casualties are high." I couldn't believe what I was hearing with screams and mostly unintelligible shouting. "Oh my God," I said, invoking God's name in such a prayerful cry for the first time in my life. I listened in shocked silence knowing that my friends, including Utah, were under serious attack. The fighting and sounds stopped after another ten minutes. Several Medevac choppers were dispatched to the site to bring back the wounded.

We learned that three soldiers had been killed that night, including Private Bob Haynes who was working my radio on the inside of the perimeter where I would have been. Bob was the first one killed when a mortar round landed close to where he was positioned. I was stunned and grief-stricken for this man. Why? Why did this killing happen? Death was now so real to me. Bob had been a friend. At least ten other soldiers were injured and medevac'd out that night. Utah was safe. One of the survivors lost parts of his arms and legs. Later, one of our guys visited him in the hospital, and the sight of our comrade as an amputee made him physically sick.

Over the next weeks, I tried my best to make sense out of what had happened. Bob Haynes was carrying my radio, and he was tragically killed. I grieved over his death with pangs of guilt. I kept asking why? Why him and not me? The circumstances that allowed me to be out of harm's way and in the rear area were highly unusual—even mysterious. Two of us were flown out that morning leaving the rest of the company behind. In all my time in Vietnam, before and after that event, I do not ever recall any sick people being flown back to the rear area. The only reasons a combat soldier left the field were because he was seriously wounded and needed hospital treatment or because he was re-assigned, for example, to another job or to go back to the states. Why did the captain send me back that morning? I had no rational explanation, but my mind was full of perplexing questions. Was this merely a case of my good luck that I was flown to safety only a few hours before the deadly attack? Was the hand of God somehow involved with my life being spared? And, if so, why? Is God even capable of such intervention? And why me? I had many questions but no answers.

When I went to Vietnam in 1969, I was a self-described agnostic—not an atheist, mind you, but someone who wanted proof that God existed before I would believe. The circumstances surrounding this event challenged my thinking. My life was not any more or less valuable than Private Haynes's life, but some sort of random good luck made no sense whatsoever. There was no lottery drawing as to who could return to the rear area. There were so many different parts of this event that had to come together to allow my return to the rear area—my severe illness and temperature that I never again experienced in my tour of duty, the precise timing of our weekly supply helicopter arrival, the highly unusual decision made by our captain to put two of us on that chopper—that I came to the only conclusion that seemed even remotely rational. I was divinely protected during this deadly attack. At that point in my life, this conclusion sounded so outrageous and preposterous to me that I never would have thought to share it with anyone. And I didn't. The difficult questions for me still far outweighed any rational answers. But my mind was opened to the possibility of an intervening God because of this experience.

This letter is rather upbeat even though it was written at a sad time just after the attack that killed my friend Bob Haynes. I knew any mention of the event to Connie would only be cause for great worry. And, of course, I was still processing this tragedy.

Each morning we had to pack up any gear we had used and prepare to move out. We would often trek through open fields and rice paddies to nearby thatched-hut villages to see if there were any Viet Cong there or any evidence of their presence. We would walk maybe three or four klicks (a klick is one kilometer, about 2/3 of a mile) and check out an area or a village. Many days I had the impression that we were walking guinea pigs, trying to get the enemy to show themselves and attack us so we could call in our superior air power and destroy their strongholds. One morning after humping a couple of hours to a small village, we arrived about 10:00 a.m. and came upon three Marines who were standing around and drinking beers. Since I was such a clueless rookie, I foolishly tried to poke fun at these guys. I said to them., “Hey, you guys must have it pretty easy to be standing around and drinking beers at ten o’clock in the morning.” That was a serious mistake. These guys glared at me like, “Who is this crazy dude to even make such a stupid comment particularly to a Marine?” One of them angrily responded, “The three of us were up at 0500 hours this morning and sat up on a hill outside a village waiting for the Viet Cong soldiers to leave. We killed four of them. Then we trekked three klicks north to another vill and picked off two more. Then we hiked three klicks here to check out this vill. What have you guys done this morning?” Wow! That was a well-deserved punch straight to the gut. These Marines were aggressively fighting this war and constantly out seeking trouble. They thrived on this kind of dangerous military activity walking through enemy-infested territory in the dark of the night and early morning hours, a dangerous time of VC troop movement. Whoa, I thought. I have great respect for these guys. They make an everyday occurrence out of being unbelievably tough and fearless.

Black and White

A combat infantry unit to be effective—in fact to be any good at all—must operate as a cohesive team. Everyone is facing death, so it is essential that each one looks out for and protects his fellow soldier. There exists a camaraderie in combat that is highly unusual, if not unique. There is no better example of that phenomenon then the relationship between black soldiers and white soldiers. There was no racial distinction in the field with our company. A night time position is established with three soldiers in one place; each soldier depends on the other to take his turn at watch and to protect the back (and life) of his comrade. Black, Caucasian, Hispanic, or some mixture thereof made no difference because we were all working together to stay alive.

I became friends with big (6' 3" tall, 225 pounds) Cal Payton. Cal was an African-American from Newark, New Jersey. He was outgoing and a natural leader. He became, among the enlisted soldiers, the recognized head guy, "the boss." My first three weeks in country I was either hanging with Utah or off by myself reading one of several books I always carried with me. After all, I didn't want my mind to deteriorate while I was stuck in this year-long battleground.

One afternoon when we were staying for a couple of days on the beach of the South China Sea, I received word that Cal wanted to see me. He and a bunch of the guys were in a large bunker smoking and talking. Cal was using some stacked sandbags for a chair, and I had to look up at him when I walked in. "Givens," Cal called out in a patronizing tone. "Get on over here, man, join the group. Smart guy like you. I hear you got one of them Masters' Degrees. Fantastic, man! We're goin' put that baby (he used a slightly more colorful word) up on the side of this bunker and them Viet Cong ain't never gonna attack us when they find out we got someone as smart as you with us. We're so glad you're here, man." Cal continued in that derisive tone for another minute or so before I interrupted him. By that time, I actually was smiling, but contrite, and shaking my head in agreement to let him know I understood. "OK, Cal," I said. "I get it. I get it. I'm just one of the guys." After that confrontation I became friendly with Cal and enjoyed talking one on one with him on a number of occasions and topics. I learned a lot from this tough, streetwise man. Many months later, and just before Cal left country, we were both at LZ Gator in the four-seater outhouse doing our business. I told Cal how I appreciated getting to know him over these months and asked, "Say, Cal, if I see you walking down the street in Newark someday, are you going to say hi to me?" Cal's response was quick, truthful, and revealing. "It depends on who I'm with."

On the rare occasions when our company was on "stand down" in the rear area, black-white racial tensions came to life. Blacks generally hung with blacks and whites with whites. We had one fist fight between a black soldier and a white soldier and it seemed to me like sides were picked for the fight based solely on race. Unfortunately, from any objective perspective, attitudes and actions in the rear area—where soldiers were not in such life and death danger—reflected similar divisive racial attitudes prevalent on America's streets during the 1960s.

My Friend, Lt. Larry Betts

In mid-October, Second Lieutenant Larry Betts arrived in country for his first assignment after ROTC (Reserve Officer Training Corps) at the University of Nebraska. I was assigned as his RTO and we became immediate friends. Larry was not one of those ROTC officers who came to Vietnam needing to prove they are just as tough as the officers who graduated from Officer Candidate School. He was willing to listen to and learn from some of the trusted enlisted men who had been in country for almost a year, but he was certainly not intimidated by them. He got to know those under his command and cared about them.

Infantry officers were in charge and had great responsibility for human life when we were in the field. Their accurate assessment of situations and their actions easily could make the difference between life and death. Most of the enlisted men understood and respected that a combat officer was under an immense amount of pressure leading troops in these dangerous situations. However, the military formalities prevalent in stateside bases didn't apply in combat. Nobody, for example, ever saluted. Larry and I were close in age, older than the average soldier. We had plenty in common being college graduates and married. We spent a lot of time together in his short time in country and were able to joke around with each other. He was someone I would be friends with at home. I wrote to Connie saying how glad I was to be working with someone like Larry and said, "He is a friend and a really good man."

In this letter I mention to Connie that a new Lieutenant (our new platoon leader) arrived in camp and I was assigned to carry his radio. His name is Larry Betts and we quickly became friends. I also talk about the rice paddies we walk through which now, in monsoon season, are filled with water.

On November 21, 1969, our company was walking narrow, overgrown trails through the fields in Quang Ngai Province. Bravo platoon was walking lead that day and Larry, unlike some officers, chose to walk the point. We were alert to the fact that the Viet Cong (VC), often put booby traps on these kinds of paths because the brush could hide the wires. So, Larry warned us about that danger, and he was proceeding slowly. Every infantry company employed an interpreter; Bo, a fifteen-year-old South Vietnamese boy was that person for us. Bo was a gregarious, high-energy person, and he quickly moved ahead of us saying, "Lieutenant, you are moving too slow." I was walking ten feet directly behind Larry.

Our interpreter hurried past us and less than a minute later inadvertently tripped a wire stretched across the path that was attached to a hand grenade. Bo kept on moving unaware that he had tripped the wire. Larry was only a few feet away when the grenade exploded. The sharp metal fragments shot out from the detonated grenade. Larry turned around slowly, his eyes rolled up, and he fell to the ground. I could see that he caught much of that shrapnel on his body. I immediately called for the medic and then called in a Medevac helicopter. Larry had gone into shock before we loaded him on the helicopter. Within thirty minutes, we learned that he had been pronounced DOA (Dead on Arrival) at the hospital in Chu Lai. It was as if all the air was suddenly sucked out of me when I received that notice. What a terrible and personal loss to all of us who knew him.

Once again, my life had been spared, this time by only a few steps. If Bo hadn't passed us, Larry would have been walking point, and he might have inadvertently tripped the wire. I would have been the one hit with the shrapnel. I was particularly devastated by Larry's death—so young, happily married, and such a good man and friend. As a result of this tragedy, unexplainable questions again arose in my mind. Why Larry and not me? What sense can be made from such a tragic death? Why would God allow this tragedy to happen to such a good man? I tried without much success to process these thoughts.

In 2001, almost thirty-two years after this tragic event, I would go searching for and meet with Larry's wife and family. The thought of finding Larry's wife came to me as I was reading a Tom Clancy novel where the main character, Jack Ryan, meets the wife of a soldier killed in Vietnam. It was as if a flash of light went off in my head. I knew Larry was happily married and living in Nebraska when he entered the service. Why had I never tried to reach his wife? I was with her husband before he died. I knew exactly what happened and I knew that he did not suffer. Maybe those details would be informative and of some comfort to her. I determined that I would locate Larry's wife. Of course, what would happen after I found her would be more up to her than to me. The ensuing story is both fascinating and inspiring in so many aspects.

I started with what I knew about Larry and what I could find on-line. Even though I knew he lived in Nebraska, his military records listed him from Eagle River, Alaska, where apparently he had lived at one time. I checked newspaper articles and then contacted the newspaper in this town in Alaska without any success. Next, I went to a website that listed everyone killed in Vietnam and found that Nebraska City, Nebraska, was listed as his home town. I started by talking with someone at the local newspaper who had some information about Larry including finding his obituary. They suggested that a woman at the local library may have additional information. This woman found some information on Larry but, more importantly, she asked if I had talked to Larry's aunt, Mrs.

Everett Haith, in Nebraska City. When I said no, she gave me a phone number for Mrs. Haith. She encouraged me by saying, "You'll want to talk with her." Small towns are often wonderfully friendly and helpful with this kind of local knowledge.

I was busy at work and it was a few days before I was able to make the call. "Mrs. Haith," I said over the phone, "my name is Bob Givens; I knew your nephew, Larry, in Vietnam and I'm trying to locate Larry's wife." "Oh, my," she replied. "I have been expecting your call; the people at the library alerted me so I wondered when you would phone me. And call me Shorty, everybody does." She was close to Larry as he grew up and he lived with her for a period of time in Nebraska City. It was one of those phone calls where after fifteen minutes it felt like we had known each other for years. She even invited me to come visit her. She told me how the Nebraska City council built a memorial to locals who were killed in Vietnam. They were not going to include Larry because he technically was from another town, although he had lived with Shorty for a time. Shorty was friendly but tough. Don't get her mad! The town leaders didn't stand a chance against this dynamo trying to justify their actions. As you might expect, Larry's memorial sits in a garden in Nebraska City.

About thirty minutes into our conversation Shorty blurted out, "Oh, I bet you don't know." "Don't know what," I asked curiously. She told me, "Larry has a son—Larry Junior." I was so shocked at that news that I couldn't say anything. Shorty explained to me that on the same day Larry was killed in Vietnam, his wife Diana found out that she was pregnant. I realized that, of course, Larry never knew that Diana was pregnant. If he did, he would have shared that great news with me. After leaving the doctor, Diana went to her art class at the University of Nebraska. The image of the two soldiers who came into the classroom and called Diana out was a blur to her. "We're sorry to inform you ..." And the rest of the words, telling her Larry had been killed in action, were unintelligible to her. I had tears in my eyes as Shorty told me about Diana's ordeal and this sad, sad story. Of course, I can give you the phone number for Diana and for his son "Little Larry". Shorty told me they both live in the Phoenix area.

I decided I would talk with Larry Jr. first and see if he was receptive to my search to meet both him and his mother. When I phoned to tell him of my search and conversation with Shorty, Larry was very interested and pleased to hear from someone who had served in Vietnam with his biological father. He assured me his mother would welcome talking with me and said he would alert her to my upcoming call. I waited a day or two to call Diana. When I reached her, she listened to my story about locating her through Shorty and seemed genuinely happy to receive my call. After a few minutes of getting acquainted on the phone, I told Diana that I would be coming to Phoenix for business in early November and wondered if it would possible to meet her and Larry Junior for lunch. The truth was that my business meetings were in Boise, Idaho, over 900 miles away from Phoenix. But I thought it might scare Diana to say I was flying into town just to meet her and Larry. I made reservations at a luxury Phoenix hotel and we made plans to meet there for lunch.

I arrived in Phoenix the day before our scheduled luncheon. I had time to play some tennis and get to know some of the hotel workers and restaurant wait staff. When I told them about my upcoming meeting, they were all fascinated by the story; it seemed practically everyone in the hotel was involved with and excited about the prospect of my meeting with Larry's wife and son thirty years after the tragic death of the husband/father. Naturally, I was excited anticipating this meeting but also just a bit apprehensive. I didn't want them to think that I was some sort of strange, crazed, fifty-five-year-old war veteran looking for "who knows what." I made sure she knew I was the president of a successful software company to try to relieve any concerns about my personal motives.

I stood outside the restaurant waiting for Diana. As she approached, I held out my hand to greet her; Diana ignored my hand and gave me a nice hug. She introduced me to "Little Larry," his wife Melissa, and to Norm, her husband of almost twenty-eight years. Norm had actually been a friend of Big Larry's in Nebraska. Our conversation flowed easily over the next ninety minutes. She had received some inaccurate information from the Army about Larry's death. I was able to describe exactly what happened that day back in 1969 and give them assurance that Larry did not suffer before he died. I gave Larry Junior a copy of a letter I had written to my wife just before Larry's death. The letter described my new friend, 2nd Lt. Larry Betts and what a "good man he was." I also gave them a picture of Larry and me taken a couple of weeks before his death. We talked about many other things during lunch including their continued interest in Nebraska football (something hereditary for Nebraskans, I believe), and other outdoor interests. As we parted with hugs and handshakes, I said that I hoped Larry was looking on and pleased with our reunion. Surprisingly for me—someone who has few if any lingering issues from Vietnam—this meeting with Diana and "little" Larry provided a nice sense of closure and fulfillment.

Over the ensuing years, I have stayed in touch with Diana and Norm and Larry and Melissa. To make this kind of relationship happen, it seems there always needs to be one person on each side who is diligently communicative. Melissa is one of those people. We most recently met for breakfast in Phoenix in early December 2018. Connie and I were celebrating her brother Dale's seventy-fifth birthday the next day. We renewed our friendship and even met the next generation of Betts's, Larry III and Maddie, who skipped school to come learn about their grandfather and a little bit about the war in Vietnam. It was a wonderful reunion.

July 27, 1969
1:55 P.M.

Dear Con,

On the last page of this letter are some notes I made the night we came into Vietnam, I scribbled them out so you would know what time I left and got here, etc. Right now I am in Chu Lai, which is up North. I have been assigned to the Americal Division -- which doesn't mean anything to me either. I do <u>not</u> as yet have an address where you can write me. I will process tomorrow and get paid. Then probably Tuesday or Wednesday we'll start our 7 days of training here. "Here" is the Americal base camp replacement station. After this training we'll be assigned to a unit.

The weather here is very hot, muggy, and ("you guessed it") "stuffy." It seems to rain every day, but that doesnt help much. Yes-terday after we reached Chulai (by military plane), we went swimming in the ocean. The beach is about 20 yards

PRETTY APPROPRIATE, EH?
"ARE YOU SURE YOU'RE NOT A.W.O.L.?"

(2)

from my barracks. The nights are hot and we don't use blankets or sheets. I certainly didn't expect to be swimming in VN., so that was a pleasant surprise. Today (for the 2nd time) I'm on K.P., and it is a real pain. On this particular base camp, there is a club for enlisted men, a movie every night, swimming, PX, sandwich stand, laundry, and Chapel. It is pretty safe, and as you can tell, fairly well equipped.

The first day I had K.P. there were several Vietnamese "Mamasons" (women) working and a couple talked pretty good English. They were talkative, and not really shy. One was teaching me some Vietnamese, and I was able to pick it up pretty well. I might try and take a course in Vietnamese while I'm here. Oh, also on this base are Kit Carson scouts. These are people who formerly fought for the N.V.A. or Vietcong and who came

(3)

over to our side. All the VN people are small, but the Kit Carson scouts are about 5'0" and look like 15 or 16 year olds

You don't need to send me a watch. Last night a fellow gave me a watch he had found buried in the sand. It's not bad – a Rodania – with a Speidel twist-o-flex band.

I will write when I have more news, and will send my address as soon as I can. I hope you enjoyed your trip, even tho I'm sure it was a little difficult. So now, since I'm fighting for you, how about getting a job for me? O.K. I love You!

"HOLD IT! THIS ONE IS THE GARBAGE. THAT ONE IS TONIGHT'S BEEF STEW."

Love,

Bob

I won't be able to give you my address for 7 or 8 days.

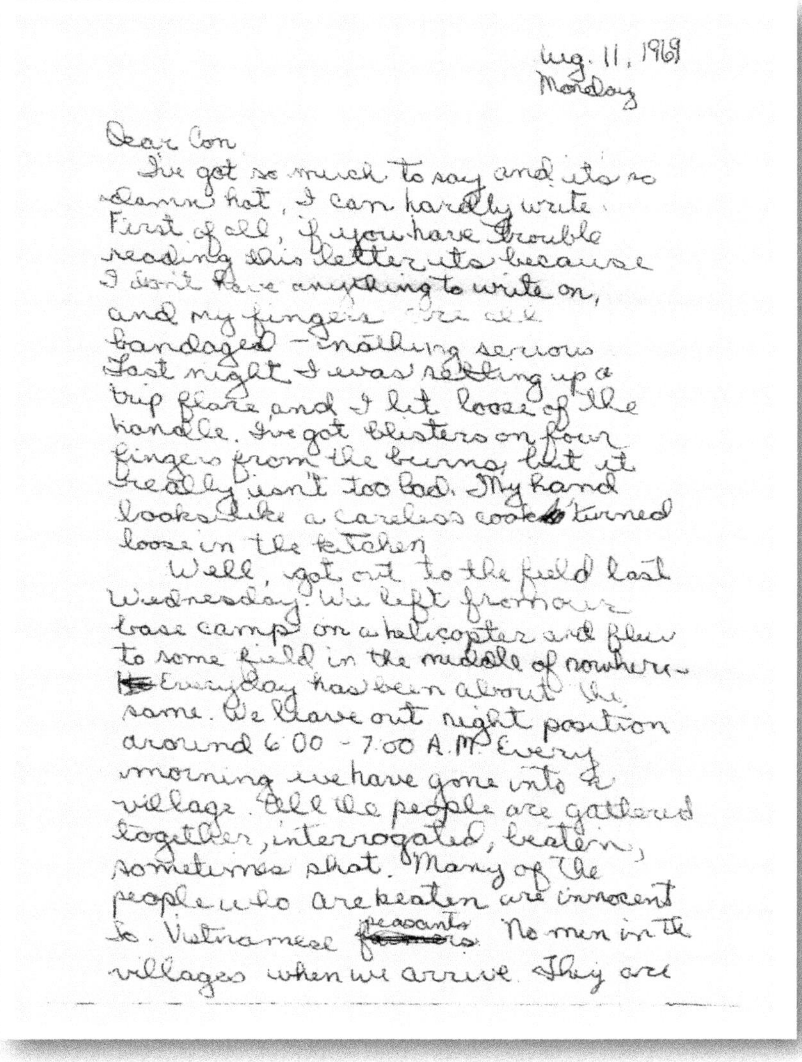

Aug. 11, 1969
Monday

Dear Con
I've got so much to say and it's so damn hot, I can hardly write. First of all, if you have trouble reading this letter its because I don't have anything to write on, and my fingers are all bandaged — nothing serious. Last night I was setting up a trip flare and I let loose of the handle. I've got blisters on four fingers from the burns, but it really isn't too bad. My hand looks like a careless cook turned loose in the kitchen.

Well, got out to the field last Wednesday. We left from our base camp on a helicopter and flew to some field in the middle of nowhere. ~~He~~ Everyday has been about the same. We leave out night position around 6:00 - 7:00 A.M. Every morning we have gone into a village. All the people are gathered together, interrogated, beaten, sometimes shot. Many of the people who are beaten are innocent S. Vietnamese ~~farmers~~ peasants. No men in the villages when we arrive. They are either fighting for the South or with the V. C. We stay in the village until late afternoon, and then go to our night position. It's hot, dirty, and seems so senseless.

I'll tell you more later, except that we will be in the field until Sept. 1, and then we go back to guard our base camp for a month. That won't be so bad, because we can take a shower and sleep on a cot and eat hot meals. I'll be able to write you better then, and also get off a letter to Mom & Dad. I'm sure I won't write them until that time, so maybe you can give them my address.

Quite frankly this whole business is so disgusting that I find myself very discouraged much of the time. The only thing I have to look forward to are your letters. At least until R and R gets closer or next July. Let's hope the time goes a little faster.

When you write me, will you send me a package (one) of pre-sweetened Kool-Aid. Also every 2nd or 3rd letter, enclose an envelope and a couple of sheets of paper. If I carry paper with me in the field it just gets wet.

→

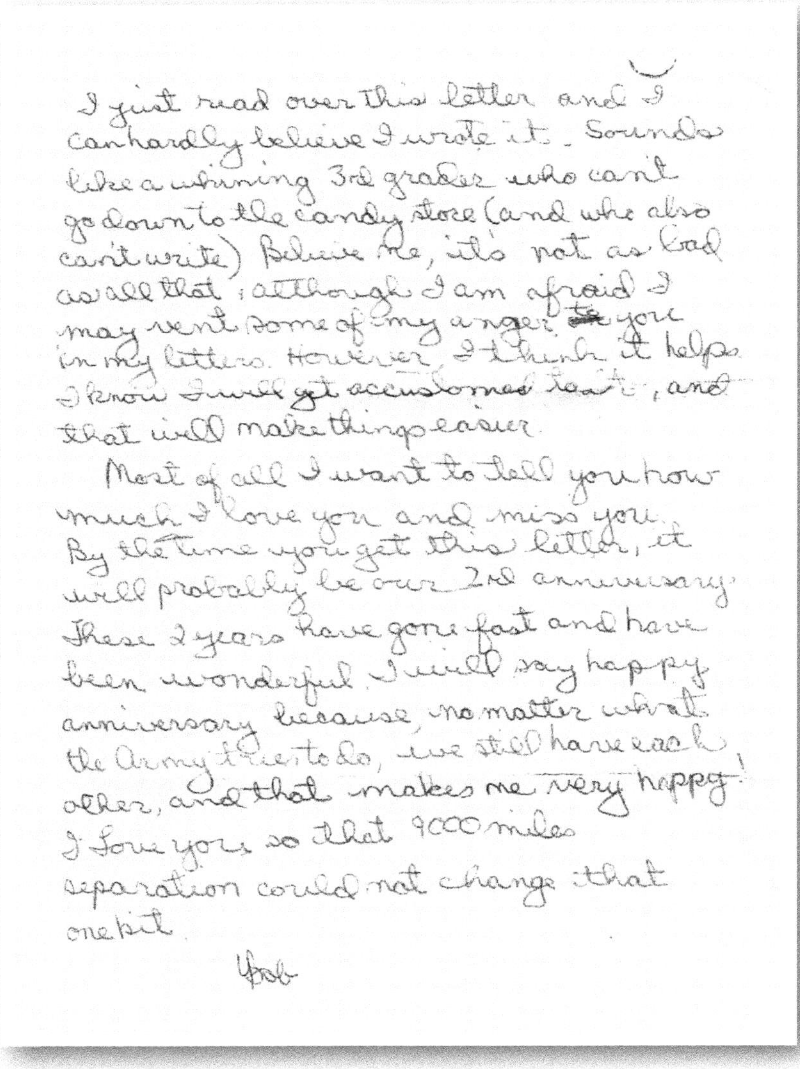

I just read over this letter and I can hardly believe I wrote it. Sounds like a whining 3rd grader who can't go down to the candy store (and who also can't write) Believe me, it's not as bad as all that; although I am afraid I may vent some of my anger ~~to~~ you in my letters. However, I think it helps. I know I will get accustomed to it, and that will make things easier.

Most of all I want to tell you how much I love you and miss you. By the time you get this letter, it will probably be our 2nd anniversary. These 2 years have gone fast and have been wonderful. I will say happy anniversary because, no matter what the Army tries to do, we still have each other, and that makes me very happy! I love you so that 9000 miles separation could not change that one bit.

Bob

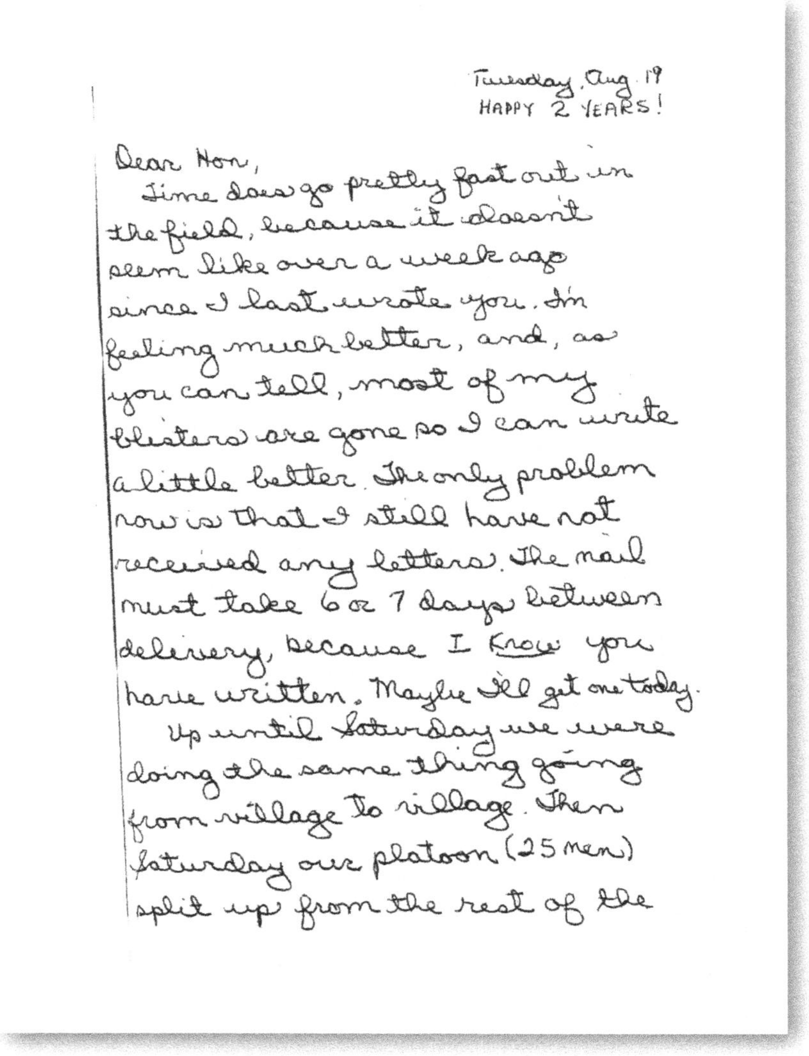

Tuesday, Aug. 19
HAPPY 2 YEARS!

Dear Hon,
Time does go pretty fast out in the field, because it doesn't seem like over a week ago since I last wrote you. I'm feeling much better, and, as you can tell, most of my blisters are gone so I can write a little better. The only problem now is that I still have not received any letters. The mail must take 6 or 7 days between delivery, because I Know you have written. Maybe I'll get one today.

Up until Saturday we were doing the same thing going from village to village. Then Saturday our platoon (25 men) split up from the rest of the

(2)

company, and we are now on some peninsula right on the coast. All we have been doing is sending out patrols around this area. In the afternoon, we go swimming (skinny-dipping) in the So. China Sea. So this particular mission is not too bad. Yesterday after we got out of the water, we saw 4 N.V.A.'s (No. Vietnamese Army) swimming about 500 meters up the coast from us. A patrol was sent out but they didn't find them in time. As far as I'm concerned there's plenty of room for everyone to swim.

In the two weeks I've been in the field, I have not seen one N.V.A. or V.C. (I didn't see those 4 swimming yesterday, because I was cooking my dinner at that time)

(3)

However, most of the time they watch where you go, where you set up camp, etc. The person who watches is an enemy sniper, and he may be in a tree, or underground in one of their many tunnels. At any rate, they are almost impossible to spot. We have received sniper fire 3 or 4 times, and have been in one fire fight. A sniper usually fires just one burst and then takes off. If we are walking, we all hit the ground and fire in the direction of the sniper (not knowing exactly where that is) If we are in our N.D.P. (night defensive position) we get in our foxholes and return fire. The fire fight is a little worse, because as I said snipers

(4)

generally fire and run, causing harassment more than anything else. In the fire fight there were several enemy firing on us, and we had a 15 minute shoot out. I didn't see any enemy, however, because I hit the ground and only looked up to fire a round or 2 in the direction of the enemy. Our Commanding Officer then called in gunships (helicopters with rockets, mortars, machine guns) and they ran the enemy off. After it was all over there were no injuries on our side and apparently none on theirs either. So that should give you some idea of what goes on, and as you can tell most days nothing happens. Even when something breaks out the enemy is usually so far away that it is hard for anyone to get hit. The

(5)

reason, it seems to me, that we do get to them and not vice versa is that we have the "choppers" and planes to chase them down, and once they spot the enemy the aircraft are pretty effective. Enough of that - unless you are particularly interested you can ask me about it in your letters which I <u>Know</u> are on their way!

I believe I mentioned we will be in the field until Sept. 1, and then go back to our base camp for the month of September. This month is the best time to send me things because I can keep them in my foot locker. So any books magazines, etc. try to get them to me before Sept. 30. Incidentally I'm making more requests in this letter, and I probably will in most of my letters. I don't

(6)

really mean to keep you
running around getting stuff
for me all the time, but I think
that if I keep up an energetic
schedule of reading, studying, et
the time will go faster. I also
find that I am much less
bored if I am undertaking some
kind of project. Therefore
(Besides my previous requests)
I want to start reading on the
stock market and investing.
Any material you can send would
be good. I believe it would be
most beneficial if you could
find a sort of "Beginners - introduction
to the basic operation of the stock
market and a beginners guide to
investing." In other words, I'd like
to start from the bottom and get
some of the fundamentals before
getting too technical. I would

(7)

suggest 2 sources (1) your friend at the public library (2) any investment firms in the R.I. area. Now, they probably have propaganda material (which is O.K.) but also they might suggest reading material for someone interested in learning about the market.

Also I would like to request 2 more books:

(1) Brave New World, Huxley
(2) Steinbeck (Either Travels with Charly and/or one which you already have that I might like)

Now anything that you send should be wrapped in a plastic (preferably heavy) bag. For example, kool aid and writing paper in "baggies."

Also we get pipe tobacco out here, but I have no pipe. Maybe you can take care of that, too.

Also any puzzles (Reader's Digest vocabulary, Sports Quizzes, etc.) would be nice to keep me occupied.

(8)

Now -
after reading this far and thinking maybe I want the Library of Congress shipped over plus all its gift shops, you should probably sit down, grab a cold coke, and wonder whether slavery was abolished (or "who was your servant last year") - Incidentally, if you can ship over the Library of Congress, make sure it arrives between Sept. 1 and the 30. . . !!?

I won't add that I'm anxious to hear how you are, what you've been doing, how much you love me, how much you miss me, how long this year is going to be, how you don't know what you're going to do without me for the next 340 days, whether you have found a job, whether you're broke, who you have seen, and who you

(9)

have heard from... because I know that you have told me all these things and the letters are on their way right now.

I will add that I am fine, I am out here in the field in sunny Vietnam, I love you very much, I miss you more every day, I am sure this is going to be the longest year in recorded history, I don't know how I'm going to get along without you for the next 340 days, I've found a job (Army dog-faced soldier), I'm not broke (won a little bit in poker), I haven't seen any old friends here, and, as of yet, I haven't heard from anyone. But I'm waiting impatiently.

All my love,

Bob

P.S. This has got to be the longest letter ever written!

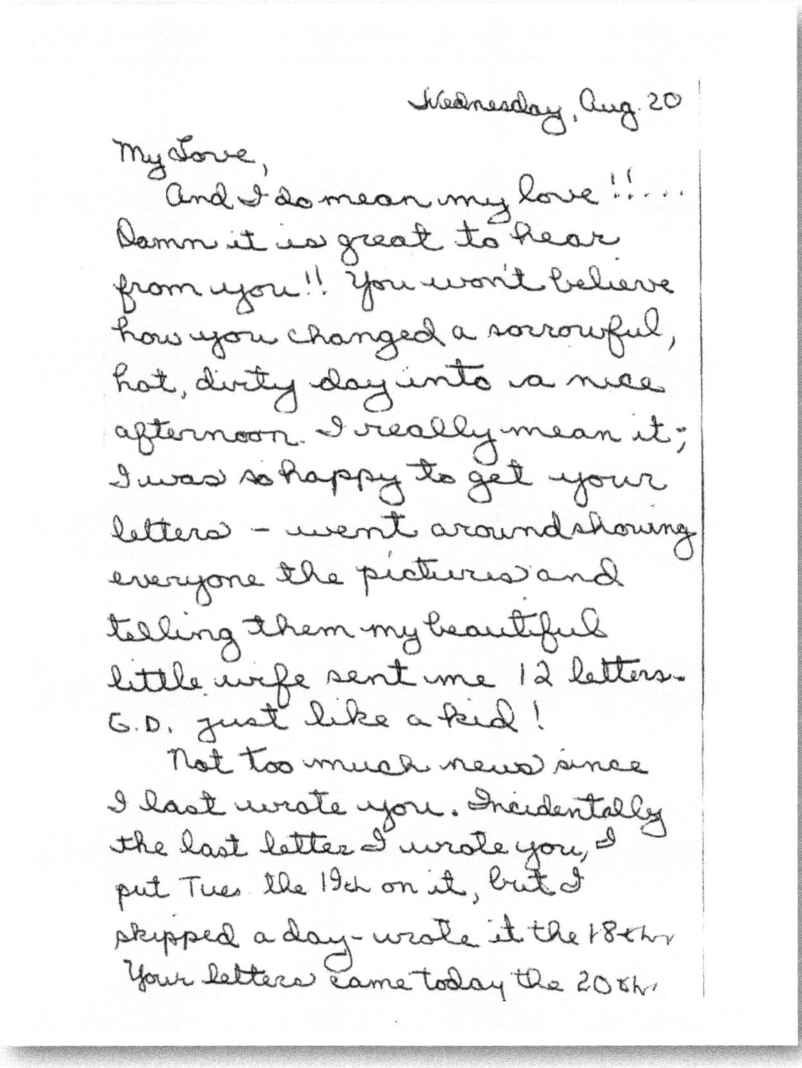

Wednesday, Aug. 20

My Love,

And I do mean my love!!....
Damn it is great to hear from you!! You won't believe how you changed a sorrowful, hot, dirty day into a nice afternoon. I really mean it; I was so happy to get your letters – went around showing everyone the pictures and telling them my beautiful little wife sent me 12 letters. G.D. just like a kid!

Not too much news since I last wrote you. Incidentally the last letter I wrote you, I put Tues the 19th on it, but I skipped a day – wrote it the 18th. Your letters came today the 20th.

Yesterday I volunteered to be R.T.O. (radio telephone operator) for the platoon. It may be only temporary, but I kind of like it. I also found out today that we will be going back to our base camp on Sat. the 23rd. That means we will probably start our bunker guard then (23rd) and stay at the base camp until around Sept. 15th. As I mentioned previously, that's a pretty decent spot - much nicer than the field. As for the packages and things, just send them when you can. It takes at least 2 weeks for a package to get here, but if one comes

The next few pages are skipped as I talk about college loan paybacks and banks …

(6)

Also you might send Yo and Lib one of those pictures. I'm going to send them back because I'm not sure if you have duplicates and also they will get ruined here. Any that I will keep here (a few with you in them-) should be plastic laminated before sent. But, I will send most back since I can only save a few.

Well, my love, it's getting too dark to write much more. You know I consider myself very fortunate to have such a wonderful wife. I love you very much.

Love,
Bob

P.S. You didn't say whether you received the $120 I sent besides

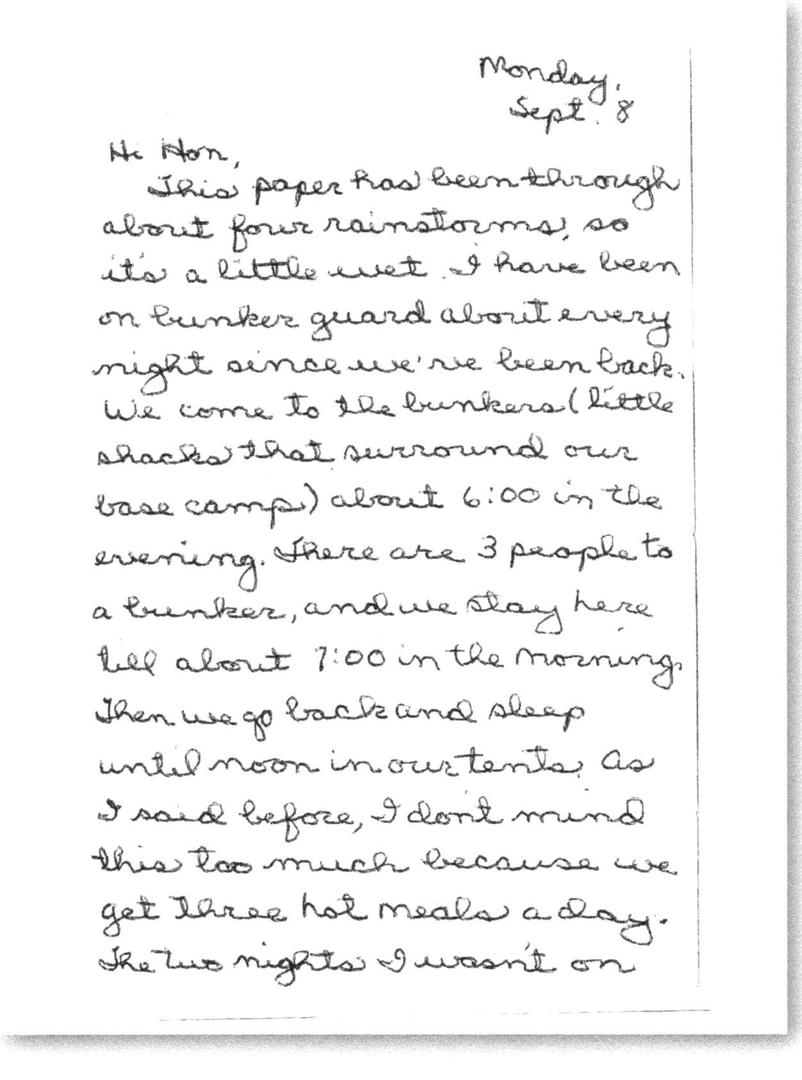

Monday,
Sept. 8

Hi Mom,
This paper has been through about four rainstorms, so it's a little wet. I have been on bunker guard about every night since we've been back. We come to the bunkers (little shacks that surround our base camp) about 6:00 in the evening. There are 3 people to a bunker, and we stay here till about 7:00 in the morning. Then we go back and sleep until noon in our tents. As I said before, I don't mind this too much because we get three hot meals a day. The two nights I wasn't on

(2)

bunker guard I went to the
EM club and they showed
movies (and served cold beer)
They showed Bullet and the
Hell Fighters (John Wayne).
Our schedule - as rumor
has it .. and you know how
that can change - looks like
we will only be here until
September 15. Then the 16th we
are supposedly going back
out to the field for about a
month. Around the 15th of
Oct., we come back in for
Stand down. Stand down is
3 days of drinking and
loafing. After that I don't
know yet. I've been
vascillating between feeling
pretty good and then a little

(3)

down. If I think too much about how much longer I have to go or how useless this all is, I get kind of depressed. But otherwise, I feel pretty good and just keep marking off the days.

Two things that I some-times took for granted, I definitely miss over here. One is that there is really no one to talk to. I don't really think of any of these guys as close friends, and I miss talking or listening to someone about subjects other than the Army, sex, and cars - which is about all they ever talk about. Like in A.I.T. with Yo, and Lib we would have some

(4)

interesting talks. I honestly think I'm too old and too serious minded to be over here; I can't seem to take wasting time the way these guys do. The second thing I was thinking about the other day is that I really haven't had a good laugh since I've been here. I know that sounds funny (odd), but like when we're together you know we enjoy doing things together and we always have a good time. By laughing, I mean that that is a symptom of a state of mind. When we're together we're happy, and as a result we have fun and laugh (sometime at ourselves) which generally

(5)

means
~~shows~~ that your happy, but
it's in a spontaneous, natural
sort of way. Here I find myself
trying to laugh, trying to find
something humorous — something
to be happy about — but you
know there is really not much.
I guess I've always tried to be
so honest with myself that
I can't really deceive myself
into thinking I'm even
somewhat happy when I'm
not. What does make me
happy though is to think
about getting home and being
with you. I'll probably be
like a little puppy dog and
just follow you around

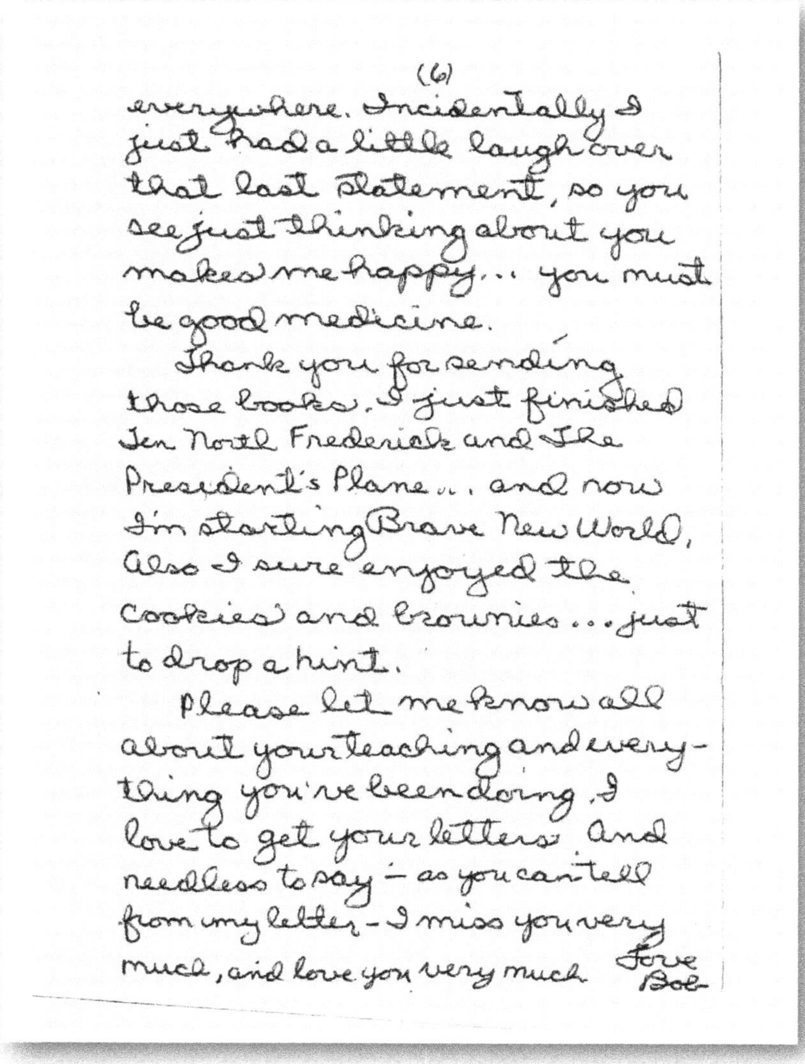

(6)

everywhere. Incidentally I just had a little laugh over that last statement, so you see just thinking about you makes me happy... you must be good medicine.

Thank you for sending those books. I just finished Ten North Frederick and The President's Plane... and now I'm starting Brave New World. Also I sure enjoyed the cookies and brownies... just to drop a hint.

Please let me know all about your teaching and everything you've been doing. I love to get your letters. And needless to say – as you can tell from my letter – I miss you very much, and love you very much.

Love
Bob

Sunday, Sept. 21

Dear Con,

Well I have a lot to tell you since my last little note I wrote you a week ago. I think I mentioned we were moving out in 15 minutes. We did — to the jungle. Sunday we flew by chopper to a place called Tra Bong. We camped there Sun. nite. Then Mon. we flew out of there to the jungle. We were only about 20 miles from the Laos border. You might be able to tell on your map; the growth was thick - called triple canopy - and the terrain was very mountainous

In triple canopy the grass and
vines are way over your head
and the trees are thick. In
many places you couldn't
even see the sky. Mon. and
Tues. were bearable because
we didn't get any rain.
Our mission was to travel
from the point where the
choppers set us down to
another point about 6 miles
away. We travelled on little
trails sometimes, and other
times had to cut our way
through with machetti's (knives)
Then Wed. afternoon the rain
came, and didn't let up
until we left Sat. morning.
It was pretty miserable.

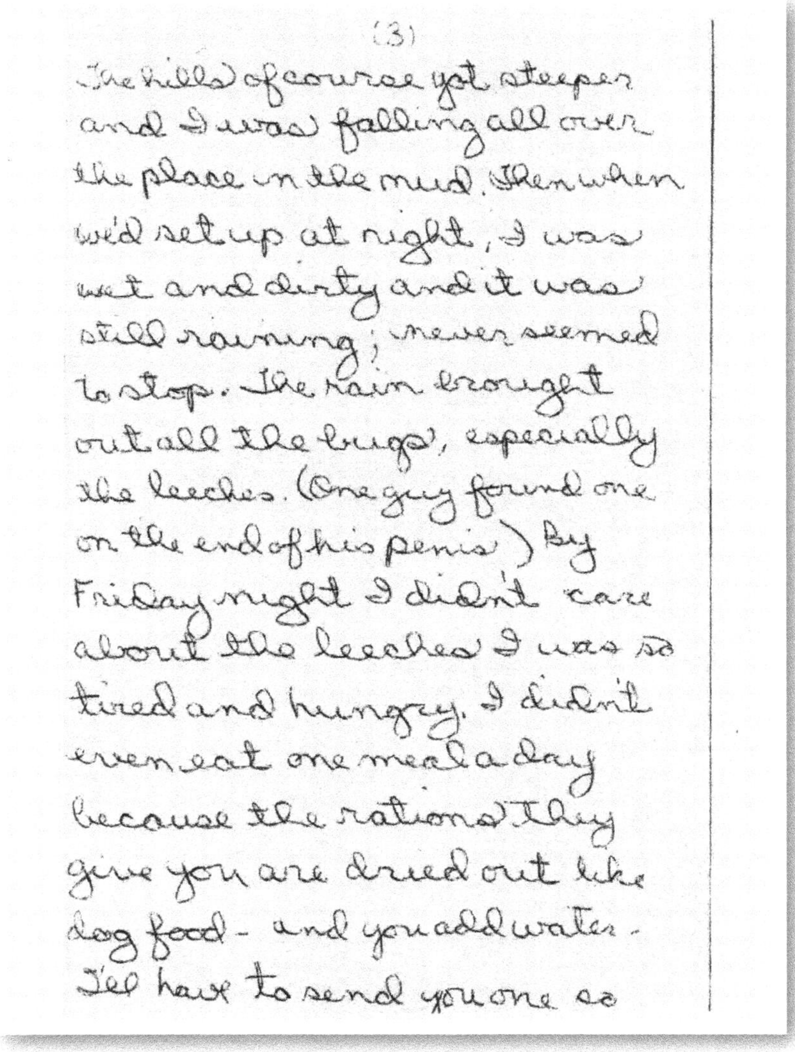

(3)
The hills of course got steeper
and I was falling all over
the place in the mud. Then when
we'd set up at night, I was
wet and dirty and it was
still raining; never seemed
to stop. The rain brought
out all the bugs, especially
the leeches. (One guy found one
on the end of his penis) By
Friday night I didn't care
about the leeches I was so
tired and hungry. I didn't
even eat one meal a day
because the rations they
give you are dried out like
dog food - and you add water.
I'll have to send you one so

(4)

you can taste it. I was damn glad to get out of that place - I hope I never see it again.

Right now we have set up camp on the So China Sea. We went back to Gator yesterday and came out this morning. I got your package and have brought all the stuff with me. Here is a rundown of the food so far:

Cookies
Brownies } Excellent - More the merrier

Wyler's Lemonade
Tea
Orange Drink
Etc. } Excellent - great stuff

Soups - Excellent
Olives - Negative
Oatmeal - looks good (haven't tried as yet)

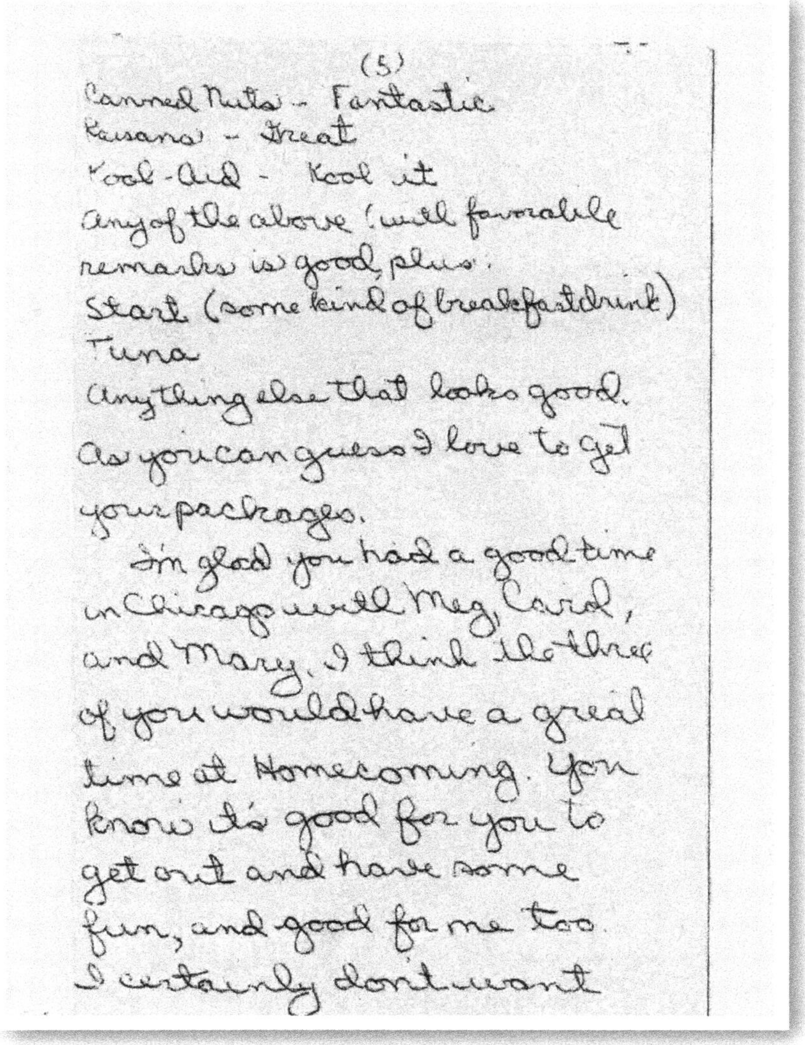

(5)
Canned Nuts - Fantastic
Raisins - Great
Kool-Aid - Kool it
Any of the above (with favorable
remarks is good, plus:
Start (some kind of breakfast drink)
Tuna
Anything else that looks good.
As you can guess I love to get
your packages.
I'm glad you had a good time
in Chicago with Meg, Carol,
and Mary. I think the three
of you would have a great
time at Homecoming. You
know it's good for you to
get out and have some
fun, and good for me too.
I certainly don't want

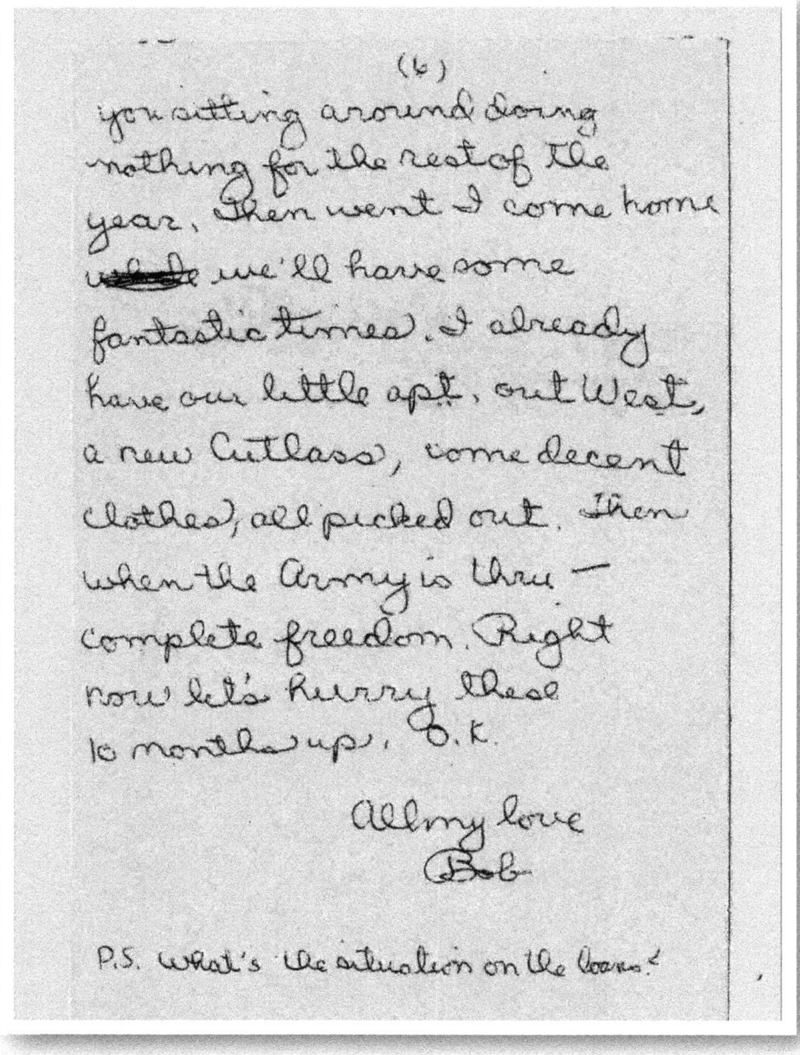

(6)

you sitting around doing
nothing for the rest of the
year. Then went I come home
~~[illegible]~~ we'll have some
fantastic times. I already
have our little apt. out West,
a new Cutlass, some decent
clothes, all picked out. Then
when the Army is thru —
complete freedom. Right
now let's hurry these
10 months up. O.K.

All my love
Bob

P.S. What's the situation on the loans?

Friday, Oct. 3
11:00 P.M.

Dear Con,

I am at Gator now (our base camp) while the rest of the company is out in the field. They are still at that Marine base camp. (135) Last Monday we moved from Cap 135 (the camp we've been set up on for several weeks) to another site. Tuesday we were supposed to go out on an ambush, but that operation was called off. So we packed up our stuff and Tuesday morning the choppers took us back to 135. I was feeling pretty rotten all that day, and the medic said my temperature was 102° - so they sent me back here. My temperature was normal the next day, but I've been having diarrhea problems - about 8 or 9

(2)

a day! So it hasn't been bad here. I've done some reading on stocks & bonds, and saw Three in the Attic yesterday. Last night, they put me on bunker guard and tonight too. The only bad thing there is that it has been raining steadily for two days now, Monsoon season. Since I'm supposed to go back to the doctor tomorrow, I may not go back out to the field before stand down. During standdown (Oct. 8-11) we move into barracks in Chu Lai (I don't know whether I told you, but at Gator our cots are in these big tents) and get steaks and relax.

(3)

I got a nice letter from Orville and Cindy yesterday - plus I got the letters from your kids. They were a riot. How about the one who said you could be as mean as a wild elephant! I will probably write a letter to the class sometime. I enjoyed reading them, and most were pretty well written.

Well, sweets, I wish I could send you something nice for your birthday. I do send all my love. Also I am starting to look into a sound system - amp, tape recorder, turntable, speakers - so I think that before I leave I will order it from the P.X. That will be like <u>our</u> birthday, Xmas, etc. It will probably run about $400.

The cake your Mom sent was very good... everybody looks forward to my packages... Happy birthday, sweet little 24.

Love,

Bob

Oct. 14, 1969

Dear Con,

Well, here I am again back out in the field. It's also one of those days where I don't really feel too much like writing. Sorry. However, I know it's been a little over a week since my last letter, and I didn't want you to worry.

Standdown was all right. We saw some "skin flicks" and a couple of stage shows. I spent most of my time in the U.S.O. in Chu Lai brushing up my ping pong game and looking for a bridge game. Never did find one tho.

We ended standdown on the 11th at about 1:30, and by 4:00 we were out in the field. This area is all rice paddies, and in places the water is as high as my navel. With the rain everyday, we are constantly wet.

Got a letter from Doug the other day. Sounds like basic is the same as it was for me. I'm going to try and write him sometime. Also, please send me Randy's address.

Rog (Utah) is the other R.T.O. for our platoon (each plt. has two) Also we have a new Lt. who is a good man. So it's not too bad being out here - at least when we're not humping and can sit around and talk.

Let me know about your plans for homecoming. I'll write more later.

All My Love,

Bob

— FIVE —

Completing My Tour of Duty

Returning to the Field

Shortly after 2nd Lt. Larry Betts' tragic death, our company returned to LZ Gator for a brief four-day stand down. Our tiny mess hall surprised us with a Thanksgiving meal—turkey, mashed potatoes and gravy, and cranberry sauce. For those of us returning from the field, anything beat eating stale food out of a can, and this meal was an unexpected treat—really a feast for us. We learned to avoid using a salt shaker (only available in the rear area) because the salt was one solid glob from the high humidity.

During our time in the rear area, I had a chance to research a location for an R&R—a one-week break soldiers were given for rest and relaxation. The Army provided flights for us to a number of destinations. Married couples could meet in Hawaii where the military provided some comfort and orientation for the spouses before their husbands arrived. I researched dates and hotels and suggested we meet in Hawaii in early February. This date concerned Connie because we would still have such a long time before I returned home, over five months. Not surprisingly, I did not want to wait. The sooner the better. As I recall, a soldier was required to have six months in country before he was eligible for R&R. I would have six months and ten days. Connie agreed (of course) and made plans with her school to get a one-week leave from her teaching assignment. These requests were almost always granted to teachers or other workers with spouses in Vietnam. I made hotel reservations at one of Honolulu's finest, the Hilton Hawaiian Village. February could not come soon enough for me.

By this time in my tour of duty, I was pretty disgusted with the way politicians were conducting the war. A lot of lives were being lost and for what reason? We were not going to win this war with our ground troops or by continuing to bomb the entire country. I wanted our leaders to stop the war and bring our soldiers home. I wasn't alone in these sentiments. In November, I sent this editorial letter to Newsweek Magazine in response to an article from General Taylor. To the best of my knowledge, it was never published.)

At night in the rear area, we were sometimes able to get a poker game going. I continued my winning ways in what occasionally became rather high stakes games. We played a crazy game called six-card MacIntosh. If you matched an "up" card you had to match the pot to stay in the game. If you matched your "down" card, they became wild cards. On at least one occasion, a soldier had to match a one-hundred-dollar pot just to stay in the game. That one bet was a full month's salary for an Army Private. During one game I won a large pot from Harvey Putterbaugh, a soldier who was about to leave country and who didn't have enough money to cover his losing bet. I asked him what else he had to pay his debt. He told me he had a new pair of fifty-dollar Florsheim dress shoes size 10D. I said, "Close enough, I'll take the shoes." I'm sure Connie was a little puzzled when she received these gently-used shoes sent to her from Vietnam. In addition, I sent her a couple of hundred dollars from my poker winnings. She was a saver, so this money would be used for a vacation when I returned home.

We were paid with Military Payment Certificates (MPCs) which looked more like Monopoly money than real money. During the course of the year, I sent Connie over three-hundred dollars in poker winnings (plus a pair of shoes.)

A few days after Thanksgiving, the Huey's (our transport helicopters) were lined up at LZ Gator to return us to the field. We were expected to be out close to thirty days before returning for a short break just before Christmas. As a general rule, we Army guys were not like the gung-ho Marines we met. The Marines were anxious for action—itching for a good fire fight, volunteering for long-range patrols to pick off some enemy soldiers, actively searching for Viet Cong tunnels and caves. For me and most (but not all) of the guys in our company, we much preferred the relative safety of the rear area. Even in our squalid landing zone we had cooked meals, cots to sleep on, and cold (or at least not hot) beer. I mean, come on! Besides a mess hall, we had a nice four-seater outhouse in the rear area, a luxury by field standards. No need to carry around our entrenching tool that we used while in the field.

The rainy season was still upon us when we headed out from LZ Gator to the field—damp, rainy, and a little cool in the evening. These deployments were always mentally tough because we were leaving "relative" safety for dangerous field conditions full of hidden land mines and Viet Cong (VC) soldiers actively using guerilla tactics to search for and attack us. Rumor had it that there was a soldier at LZ Gator who would break your forearm bone so you would be sent to the local hospital rather than returning to the field. It was said he charged fifty dollars to make a clean break. He purportedly placed ammo boxes under the wrist and elbow to protect these bones, then he dropped a thirty pound fully loaded ammo box from about ten feet in the air into the middle of the forearm. I never saw this happen, but my intuition says this type of purposeful "accident" was possible.

I received at least three letters a week from my loving wife. And twice a month she mailed me a care box with some candy, books, and food. I loved getting the beef jerky (as close to eating a hamburger as I would get) and the Kool-Aid™. The powdered Kool-Aid was helpful to mask the rusty taste of the water from the iron tablets we had to use to make the water potable. The grape flavor was the best because it was strong enough to overcome the pungent odor and poor taste of any water no matter how bad the taste. I was fortunate to have a devoted wife who looked after me as best she could. Most guys were not so lucky.

In mid-December, our company was sent to a small village south of us that we had never heard of. Our job was to clear and defend the area. We walked every square foot of the village and the surrounding area to make sure it was safe and that there were no mines or booby traps. The place was pretty much deserted by the time we arrived and inspected it. The village was the infamous My Lai, where eighteen months earlier innocent villagers had been shot and killed by some US Army soldiers. This site became known as the My Lai Massacre and, understandably, was a terrible blot on our soldiers during this war. We were never told any of the details of this horrible event until after we departed. Our job was to make sure that when the general (General William Peers) arrived at the site we had cleared the village, and our company would be surrounding the area so it would be absolutely safe for him to walk around to inspect the area. Later we read in the papers that General Peers joined the troops in the field to investigate My Lai. It was implied that this brave general put himself in the midst of dangerous combat action to investigate My Lai. Hardly ... with all the effort we made to guarantee his safety there was very little danger for him.

This letter talks about our platoon being sent on several occasions to the infamous village of My Lai to secure it for an upcoming investigation (p.2). Even a magazine sent photographers along. My sentiments are accurately expressed at the ending of the letter when I say to Connie, "It's sad, believe me."

Bob Hope at Christmas

A few weeks before Christmas, we found out that Bob Hope and Connie Stevens were going to be doing a Christmas show in Chu Lai for the troops. Chu Lai was a large US Army-built compound located about ten miles from our LZ. We were thrilled to learn that we would return for stand down during Christmas and be able to see this show. Bob Hope was a theatrical legend who had traveled throughout military sites around the world in every military action since World War II to provide comedy and entertainment to the troops. Once back at our LZ, they loaded us on two-ton trucks and brought us into a large outdoor complex with an elaborate stage. There must have been close to five-thousand troops there watching the show. He joked that with so many soldiers attending the show, was there anyone watching for enemy soldiers who might be storming this compound? Of course, Bob Hope was hilarious and we loved him. But Connie Stevens ... Well ... give me a break. We hadn't seen a female like that for many months. We encountered some Vietnamese peasant women in the field and an occasional doughnut dolly or two (Red Cross volunteer) in Chu Lai. Connie Stevens pretty much stole the show with her presence and her musical talent. She also was the object of flirtatious wise-cracks from Hope about this gorgeous woman. A thunderous roar of approval went up from the soldiers when Hope pointed to her and said, "I just wanted you guys to see what you're fighting for." We loved the show and were highly entertained during this ninety-minute spectacle. Because Hope always did research on the military base where he would perform, he was able to crack jokes that were pertinent to the audience. Most importantly, he always featured a famous, beautiful female entertainer. He certainly knew how to build troop morale.

Company Clerk

A few days after seeing Bob Hope, when we returned to the field, I heard that Jim Monteith, our company clerk, would be leaving the country the first week of January. I had gotten to know Captain Martin and the other officers, and was hopeful that I would be considered for the job. One afternoon during a break in our field maneuvers, the captain was speaking on the radio to the Executive Officer (XO) in the rear area about this job and then turned and asked me a question. "Givens," he said, "Do you type?" "Yes sir," I replied as confidently as I could while telling a bald-face lie, "forty-eight words per minute." "OK," Captain Martin replied. "On January 1st you will take over from Monteith as company clerk." I could barely believe those words. I dreamt about getting this company clerk job and even volunteered to carry a radio because I knew it gave me a better chance at the job. But I never allowed myself to think that it was a sure thing. Too many things can happen and there are only two rear area jobs in an infantry company—not good odds. If my expectations got too high, the disappointment would have been devastating. So, I was beside myself ecstatic—almost in shock that I soon would be leaving the field and going to the rear area as the company clerk. I walked around the rest of that day in a sort of zoned-out but happy fog.

What great news to share with Connie! My constant efforts to land a rear job paid off. I actually went to the rear (LZ Gator) as first the mail clerk and then would take over as company clerk in February. I also reminded Connie that I would be able to apply for R&R in late December.

December 31, 1969, was my last full day in the field. I remember the night well. The moon was full and so bright that I could easily read a book with just that natural light. We were up on a hill in an open field, and I wrote a letter to Connie sharing my joy and gratitude to be leaving the field. I quietly celebrated during the evening with Utah, who was very happy for me. I told him, "Be careful now and take care of yourself." Little did I realize that about six-weeks later, I would help take care of Utah.

It didn't take Jim Monteith, the outgoing company clerk, long to explain the duties of the company and mail clerks. There were a few other benefits that accrued to the company clerks including being exempt from nighttime duties on the perimeter lookout posts of the landing zone and no worries about having to clean the outhouses (use your imagination here!). Fortunately, after Jim showed me what to do and what things needed to be regularly typed, he didn't stand around to watch me work. Good thing since my slow "hunt and peck" typing skills would have become apparent.

During my second week on the job, Captain Martin had returned to LZ Gator for a brief meeting. I was slowly typing up some documents when I heard his voice and knew he was approaching. As he drew near, I began typing very quickly without looking at the keys like a real typist. Of course, it was all gobbledygook. "How's it going Givens," the C.O. inquired? "Fine, sir," I responded as I continued to type away at blazing speed. After he left, I ripped out the useless page and re-started the document, this time more slowly and correctly at eighteen words per minute.

We are making plans for our upcoming R&R in Hawaii in early February. Connie wanted to wait until later in my tour but I wanted to see my wife as soon as possible. A few days after moving out of the field and into LZ Gator, we came under attack. I describe that attack (where five VCs were killed inside our landing zone.) In reading this letter, I realized I was surprisingly nonchalant about the whole episode and, despite the attack, still very happy to be in the rear area.

R&R in Hawaii

Hawaii could not come soon enough for me. The first week in February, Connie and I met in Honolulu, Hawaii, for R&R. Every soldier received one-week R&R that included free military flights to such places as Hawaii and Japan. We had not seen each other since July. We had spoken to each other one afternoon for a total of three minutes on a ship-to-shore ham radio. I waited in line for over an hour to say to Connie, "I love you, over." "I love you too, over," were about the only words we said in that brief conversation, the only voice communication we had in twelve months. When I saw her bright, smiling face waiting for me in the Honolulu airport lounge, I was over-the-top ecstatic. We were so happy to be together in Hawaii, even for such a short time.

The Hilton Hawaiian Village Hotel located in Honolulu on Waikiki Beach was even better than the pictures in the brochures. Of course anything, including a blanket on the lawn, would have been posh compared to where I had been living the past six months. Connie was surprised at how so many commonplace things were exciting to me—like a flushing toilet that I had not seen in all that time, running water, and comfortable pillows. She forced me to go to the emergency room at the Tripler Army Medical Center to get treatment on some open sores on my legs. These "gook sores", as we called them, were so commonplace for infantry guys that we paid little or no attention to them. Our platoon sergeant wore one pair of socks for the entire time we were in the field before a break, almost a month. I can't imagine what kind of open sores he had on his feet and ankles when he finally washed his feet and changed socks.

We rented a Mustang convertible for the week and enjoyed every minute together. We drove around the island to see a few sites and met our friends from college, Bob and Cindy Deffenbaugh, for a day of fun and golf. Bob was a Navy pilot stationed at Pearl Harbor. They were both a great comfort and help to Connie after I flew back to Vietnam. They stayed with her so she wouldn't be alone until she left the next day. Connie and I loved our time together, but dreaded the inevitable re-separation. I was counting down the hours to myself. Connie drove me to the airport for my return flight, top down on our 1969 Mustang, while Peter, Paul & Mary's hit song, *Leavin' on a Jet Plane,"* was playing on the radio. We had tears in our eyes as we kissed goodbye for almost another six months.

Back to Vietnam

In late February our company came under another heavy attack. Several men were injured including Utah. Utah was wounded badly enough that they flew him all the way to the military's largest medical facility in Cam Ranh Bay, Vietnam. He was injured, but he had all his body parts intact and would fully recover from the wounds. I typed up the paper work for him to receive his Purple Heart Award. As company clerk, my key job was to prepare a morning report each day that accounted for the location and status of every person in our company. Every soldier's assignment and physical location had to be recorded on this official daily report. For almost six weeks. I dutifully recorded Utah on medical leave while he was in the hospital.

I gave Connie the bad news in this letter (p. 4) that Utah had been wounded in action and would be flown to a hospital in Cam Ranh Bay, Vietnam for recovery treatment

Sometime in late March, Utah notified me that he was going to be released from the hospital and would be forced to report back to his infantry unit for duty. Cam Ranh Bay had a massive military presence, and I asked him if he could find a place to live and keep low. He told me he thought he could help out in an NCO club where he had made some friends. So, the arrangement was made. Every day from March to early June, I recorded Utah on the official morning report as on temporary duty (TDY) in Cam Ranh Bay. He was one-hundred-times safer there then he would have been returning to the field. And, as long as I was company clerk, he would be accounted for (nobody really checked on these details during war time.)

In June I contacted Utah and told him he needed to report back to the company as I would be handing off my job to someone else. With about six weeks before he was to leave country, I thought he would be assigned some menial rear area jobs rather than be sent back out to the field. Ultimately, he did have to go back out to the field until he left country in July. Utah was obviously grateful for my help while he was at Cam Ranh Bay. I was quite comfortable with the potential life-saving ruse and felt that, despite the deception on my part and a certain amount of personal risk, it was worth the effort to keep my friend out of harm's way. Upon his return to the States, Utah and I met up again when we both were stationed at Fort Carson in Colorado Springs for our last few months of service, me in the finance department auditing personal financial records (ugh!) and Utah on golf course maintenance (the job I would have liked—he didn't even play golf.)

In early March, the Army closed down LZ Gator and moved our company rear-area headquarters to Chu Lai, the same place we had gone to for the Bob Hope event. Chu Lai was located about fifty miles south of Da Nang and close to Tam Ky, the largest Vietnamese city in the Quang Ngai Province. This compound on the South China Sea was a much larger Army base with many more facilities than a war-area landing zone. They even had two useable tennis courts. It was almost like being in a Stateside US Army base, except of course that we were still in a war zone. We occasionally took incoming fire from the enemy. When I finished my company clerk duties, I even had time to play a little tennis, handball, and bridge. Being in the rear, particularly a place like Chu Lai, was much better and safer than humping around the bush. I was very grateful to be out of the field and into this job Captain Martin had given to me.

In April I was put in for a promotion to Sergeant E-5 by the Commanding Officer. In order to get the promotion, I had to pass an oral exam from an interview panel composed of three infantry officers. One of the officers was our XO who often played bridge with me. I got the promotion. My bridge partner officer told me I was ranked #1 out of over forty candidates. I still had my interview swagger that had served me well in the States when seeking employment. Besides the extra money, there were a number of other benefits for an E-5 including travel and living accommodations for spouses. I went from a Private First Class (E-3) upon arrival in Vietnam to a Sergeant (E-5) in about nine months. Promotions—even legitimate ones—came faster in war situations than in peace time.

In April, I was promoted to Sergeant E-5 ... legitimately this time. I wanted to give Connie this good news by short wave radio but I was not able to get a spot in a very long line of soldiers. I also wrote to my senator, Sen. Charles Percy of Illinois, thanking him for voting against Harold Carswell for the Supreme Court Justice position. Carswell had a record of endorsing segregation. I also asked Sen. Percy to please end this war! I recall receiving a personally signed letter back from him.

Getting Short

By mid-May, the end of my tour was in sight; I could begin the sixty-day countdown. I allowed myself to begin to think often about returning home to Connie. My letters home became more and more about our life after Vietnam and what we would do. I began researching different graduate programs including law school and business school. Connie would send me information that I requested from her on different schools and different programs No internet existed in those days to make this kind of information readily available—everything came by US Mail. And, mail service was free for soldiers in Vietnam. I eventually decided that I would go to business school to work on an MBA and also use the school's placement services to find a full-time job. Another area of interest for me was cars, particularly fast, sporty ones. Our car was a three-year old, six-cylinder, 155 horsepower, cheapest model Chevrolet with no options. This Chevy had a bench front seat, and I put a seat belt in the middle seat engraved with Connie's name so she would always sit right next to me. The car had no power steering or power brakes, no air conditioning, manual roll-up windows, and not even a radio. I sent home a picture of the car I wanted to purchase when I got back, a sporty Jaguar XKE. The fact that this vehicle was a pipe dream and way out of any price range we could afford made no difference. Just the thought of buying a new car was exciting and brought me great pleasure.

80 days and counting. In previous letters, I was interested in looking at several new cars when I got home. I talked about everything from a Jaguar XKE to a Chevy Camaro. We eventually bought a sporty, new, V-8 Camaro. For some unknown reason I decided in this letter to give Connie the details around a fairly typical day for me in as company clerk.

Every so often we would take incoming artillery rounds in Chu Lai. Most of the soldiers in Chu Lai were REMFs, meaning they were rear area support people who had spent no time in the field. One day I was at lunch with Terry Fletter, our mail clerk who had been in the field with me for over five months. We heard sirens while we were eating indicating incoming rounds. The cooks and most everyone else in the mess hall quickly ran out to the bunkers located nearby. Terry and I sat calmly eating our lunch. We could tell from our field experience that these rounds were not landing even close to the mess hall. I guess it made us feel a little tougher and a little bit superior to these rear echelon people.

In June I had an opportunity to take a one-week leave. I thought, of course I would love to get away from Vietnam for seven days. Several free flights a day left from Da Nang. I passed up opportunities to fly to Taiwan and Japan. I was determined to get on the flight for Australia where English was spoken. I stayed for six days in a small hotel in Sydney and saw the beautiful opera house just before it opened. I watched tennis on grass courts, a cricket match that made little sense to me, spent time on beautiful Manly Beach, took a train ride "up country," and saw the musical *Jesus Christ Superstar*. I brought sixty-two dollars with me that lasted the entire time in Australia. As I recall, the military rate for the hotel was four or five dollars per night and a beer was maybe thirty cents (it was a different time!). I even brought a couple of dollars back to Vietnam.

I had about thirty-five days left in country after I returned from Australia. Shortly after returning, I learned from the Red Cross that my dad had suffered a heart attack and was hospitalized. I asked the Red Cross to check with his doctor and see how he was doing. The doctor said he was recovering as well as could be expected, and there was no need for me to return home. OK news for dad, but of course I was hoping they would send me home.

I was down to 26 days and counting. Connie knew about Dad's hospitalization and already had talked with the Red Cross. I told Connie I had received our State-side orders. We would be stationed at Fort Riley in Junction City, Kansas. We would have almost thirty days of leave after I returned to the States.

Like everyone else who was "short," I kept a printed calendar by my bed and faithfully crossed off each day leading to my departure. These were times that made everyone a bit nervous, especially the guys in the field. It made me nervous just thinking about the instances when guys who were short had been badly injured or killed toward the end of their tour of duty. I thought, get me home! I need to get out of this place. I could almost taste freedom.

This is one of my last letters from Vietnam. We were down to 22 days and counting. Little did I know at this time that I would be coming home early—in just a little over two weeks—on emergency leave because of my father's heart attack.

It is a sad but realistic commentary on the plight of our involvement in Vietnam, that too many leaders concur with Gen. Maxwell Taylor (Nov 10 issue). His comment that our withdrawal from Vietnam would "nullify the sacrifice of the thousands of Americans killed in action," is as illogical as the often heard slogan, "fighting for peace."

Only if one defines peace as the absence of manifest violence, and ~~then ignoring~~ ignores resultant deaths and sufferings, could one accept such nonsense. Similarly, revenge, through more violence

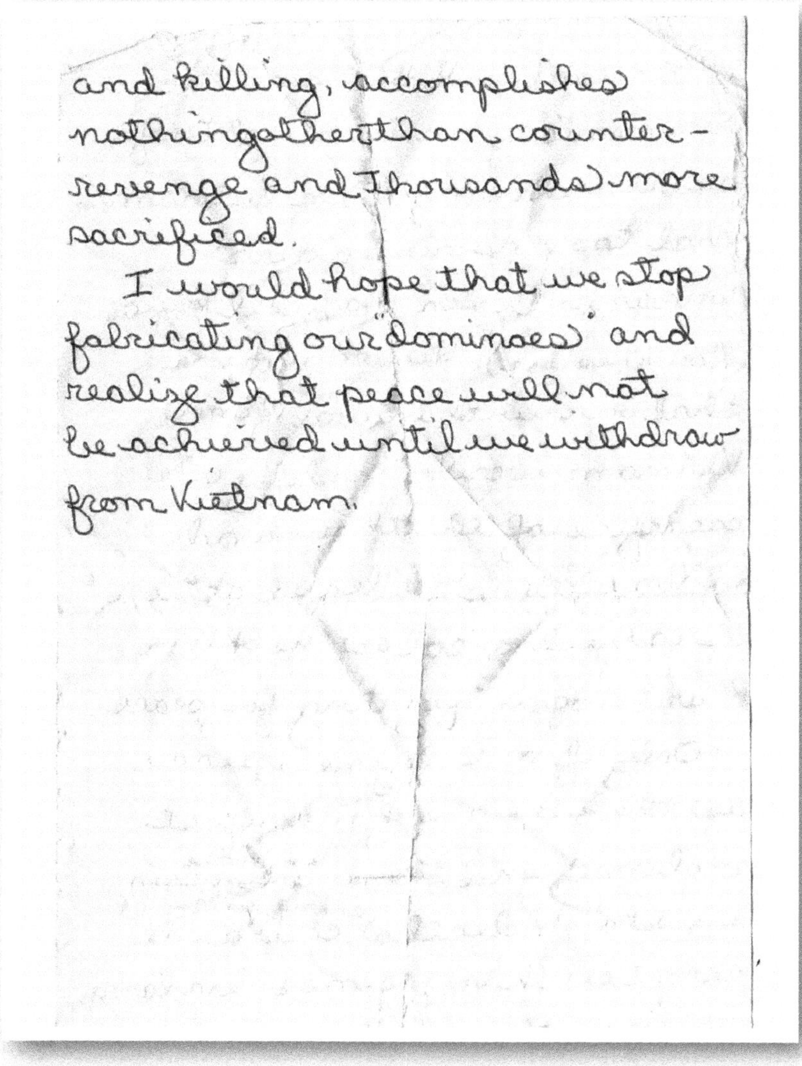
and killing, accomplishes nothing other than counter-revenge and thousands more sacrificed.

I would hope that we stop fabricating our "dominoes" and realize that peace will not be achieved until we withdraw from Vietnam.

50
50
SERIES 681
50
50

50
CENTS
50
50
CENTS
50

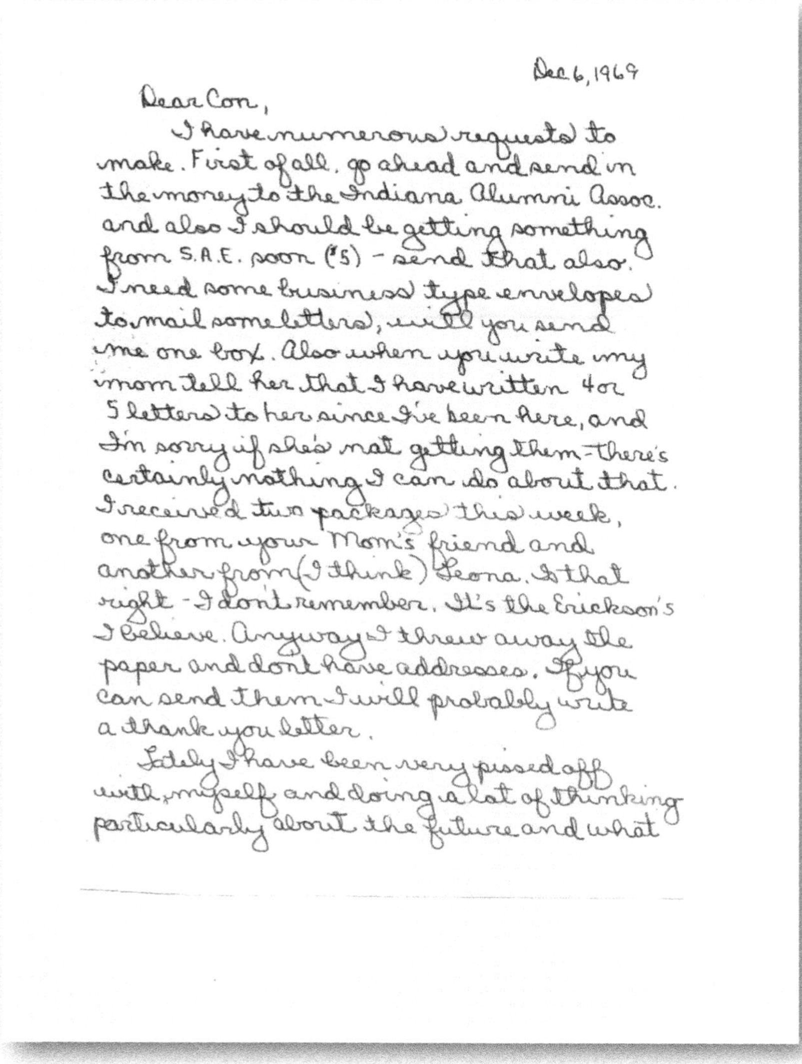

Dec 6, 1969

Dear Con,

I have numerous requests to make. First of all, go ahead and send in the money to the Indiana Alumni Assoc. and also I should be getting something from S.A.E. soon ($5) - send that also. I need some business type envelopes to mail some letters, will you send me one box. Also when you write my mom tell her that I have written 4 or 5 letters to her since I've been here, and I'm sorry if she's not getting them - there's certainly nothing I can do about that. I received two packages this week, one from your Mom's friend and another from (I think) Leona. Is that right - I don't remember. It's the Erickson's I believe. Anyway I threw away the paper and dont have addresses. If you can send them I will probably write a thank you letter.

Lately I have been very pissed off with myself and doing a lot of thinking particularly about the future and what able to do before.

There are no new developments on my job as yet, still waiting. We will be staying on bunker line for about 12 or 13 more days (till about Dec 20) which means I may not have to go back to the field.

Concerning the killings and all in the village of My Lai, we were up there about two weeks ago. In fact we have been in Pinkville on several occasions. While we were on 144, the 1st platoon from our company went into the My Lai villages with the tracks (like tanks) and secured the villages for photographers and Army officers who were investigating. There's an account of that along with other incidences in Dec. 1 issue of Newsweek. I think a lot of people (Army-type) are very uncomfortable right now. But I can certainly believe that the killings took place, and that even one deranged officer was responsible. It's sad, believe me.

Love,

Bob

Dec. 21, 1969
9:45 P.M.

Hi Hon,

Be a short letter. I'm a little "under the weather." Feels like the same thing I had last Christmas. Remember - the flu. My sinuses are a little stuffed.

Well I finally found out for sure what the hell the deal is on the job. I did get the mail clerk job for sure - first sgt. and C.O. told me today. However, I will not take over till about January 8th. So we will be going out to the field probably December 26. I will stay in the field from the 26th to about the 8th and then come back to Gator. The Company clerk and myself will be pretty much on our own back here since almost everyone else will be in the field - including C.O. and 1st Sgt.

This picture was taken in bunker control, where I work while on radio watch.

Got a letter from Bob and Cindy

today. They will be about 30 minutes from where we're staying.

Speaking of Hawaii I will be able to apply for R and R just before we go out to field, probably the 25th. It may take until the 10th - 15th to get approval and my orders. I will mail them to you as soon as I get them. You will need the orders to get a ticket at reduced rate. I should also be able to let you know what time I'll be there, were you'll meet me, where we're staying. The day is getting closer you know

All my love,

Bob

Jan. 4, 1970

Hello Love,

Please forgive me for taking so long between letters. I know I haven't written in about a week and a half. I went out to the field on Dec. 26th (The C.O. wanted me to go out as his R.T.O., because his regular R.T.O. was on a 3 day leave) I was out for 5 days and I was more nervous than usual because I knew I would be coming in soon. On Jan. 1 (a great way to start the New Year - well ... a better way) the C.O.'s R.T.O. came out and I came back to Gator. So I've been "O.J.T.ing" since I came back and have been busy trying to learn the job. Basically I have 4 jobs: Mail clerk (incoming, outgoing, money orders, etc.); training NCO (keeping records for everyone in the company on their training progress plus giving a few classes); beer and soda fund (buying and dispersing all beer & soda for company plus keeping the books); combat assault medals (recording C.A.'s

(2)

and submitting people for the medals. So, especially until I get a little experience there will be much "little stuff" to do - nothing difficult, but plenty to keep me busy. Plus last night - for the first time since last May - Gator was hit. We had some incoming mortars, grenades, small arms fire about 1:30 A.M. We had a few V.C. get through the wire and they blew up a couple of bldgs w/ satchel charges. Actually - after being in the field - it didn't bother me much, and the attack itself was pretty futile. We killed 5 V.C. and wounded several more. One G.I. was killed when his bunker caved in on him. I stayed in the Co. Area and monitored the Radio, so I felt pretty safe. Of course no place over here is totally safe, but I feel much better here at Gator than out in the field.

I'm sending letters from Ken Mitchell and Jill Gregory since I wrote them a couple of weeks ago while on bunker line.

(3)

I haven't heard anything about Hawaii yet and probably won't know definitely until Jan. 15th. As soon as I get my R and R orders I will send them. I think you should go ahead and make plane reservations for January 31st. That way you will get in Honolulu the day before (Sat), and I will make hotel reservations for the 31st through Feb. 7th. You should make plans to return (get an early flight out) on Sunday, Feb. 8th. You will need your military I.D., plus my orders to get a reduced rate - but go ahead and make them now. If my R and R orders come thru for the 1st, I will probably arrive early on Sun. the 1st. The hotel and the R and R center will be able to give you a pretty close estimate for my arrival. I will let you know where I have made reservations, and you'll have to spend the first night (Sat) by yourself. But I think that would be better than trying to get in early Sun. morning and getting

(4)

delayed. If they change my dates, I will let you know right away so you can change your plane reservations. Then I will write and change hotel reservations. As for money, bring #500 in Traveler's Cheques instead of #400 (that's after you have bought your rd. trip ticket - bring #500) I will let you know when I get confirmation on the hotel as well as R&R dates. Only about 3 weeks after you get this! Wow!

Now let me make a few comments about your last couple of letters. In the (Dec 20th) letter you talked about my two previous "heavy" letters. You said if our son had long hair vs. an education because short hair was the requirement, you would cut it. Why? Will short hair give him a better education? If a school is concerned with short hair, I personally can't see any relationship between learning and hair. And if we made our son cut his hair in order to attend that school, we would be

March 2

Hello Love,

I'm really sorry I've been so lax in writing lately. I can honestly say I have been swamped with work since I took over as company clerk. The guy who was company clerk took off for R&R the 27th and since then I have been up every night – but tonight until 12 or 1 and getting up around 4:30 – 5:30. I'm starting to get things pretty well squared away, and actually I would just as soon keep busy. Every morning at 7:00 I have to turn in a report of where everyone is, and then a morning report of any changes, reassignments, sicknesses, etc. by 9:00. That one is the real hassle because it has to be typed perfectly (in Army code and all). But I do enjoy having to use my mind a little, and once I get the routine down, it will be much easier.

The guy who's now the mail clerk and I have made a deal whereby one of us will work in the morning and the other in the afternoon, so I'll be able to play some tennis and maybe do some surfing. I hope you got my letter about sending my racquet. (W all the few letters I've written since R&R I'd hate to think you didn't get one] We have in our new company area in Chu Lai a tennis court, basketball court, handball court, about 200 yards from the U.S.O. and right on the beach. Now I really don't think that's too bad. Also - now hold on - we will have running water. I am definitely coming up in the world. You can't believe how glad I will be to get in there from Gator — let alone the field! A few people have gone into Chu Lai now to prepare the Co. area. The orderly room (me) will start~~ing~~ operating from Chu Lai on March 9th, so I'll be in there on March 8, sometime.

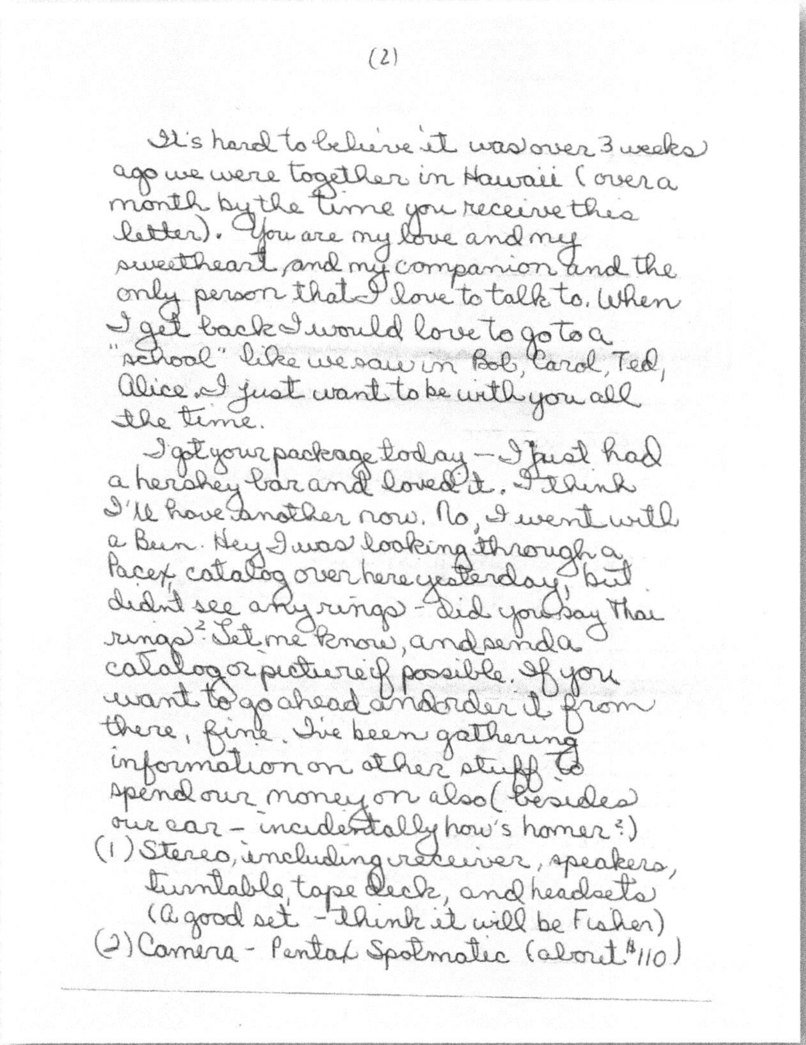

(2)

It's hard to believe it was over 3 weeks ago we were together in Hawaii (over a month by the time you receive this letter). You are my love and my sweetheart, and my companion and the only person that I love to talk to. When I get back I would love to go to a "school" like we saw in Bob, Carol, Ted, Alice. I just want to be with you all the time.

I got your package today — I just had a hershey bar and loved it. I think I'll have another now. No, I went with a Ben. Hey I was looking through a Pacex catalog over here yesterday, but didn't see any rings — did you say Thai rings? Let me know, and send a catalog or picture if possible. If you want to go ahead and order it from there, fine. I've been gathering information on other stuff to spend our money on also (besides our car — incidentally how's homer?)

(1) Stereo, including receiver, speakers, turntable, tape deck, and headsets (a good set — think it will be Fisher)

(2) Camera - Pentax Spotmatic (about $110)

(3) Movie camera & screen – maybe
But, you know, I can love you with or without
all that stuff.

I do have some bad news with all
the good things that have happened. Utah
got back from R&R about the 26th. – he
and Liz had a suite in the Hilton for $26.00
per night! and had a fantastic time. Utah
went to the field on the 26th and the
company got mortared. Utah caught
shrapnel in his back and a little in
his legs. It's a little painful right
now (he's in the hosp. in Chu Lai) but he's
doing well. He actually wishes it
was just a little worse and he would
have gone home. As it is, he will be
going to the hosp. in Cam Ranh Bay
in a few days to recover. Probably be
there 2-3 weeks. I went in to see him
yesterday and today, and he was
playing the guitar for all the patients
in his ward. He'll be O.K. Just sore
for awhile. Utah was telling me about

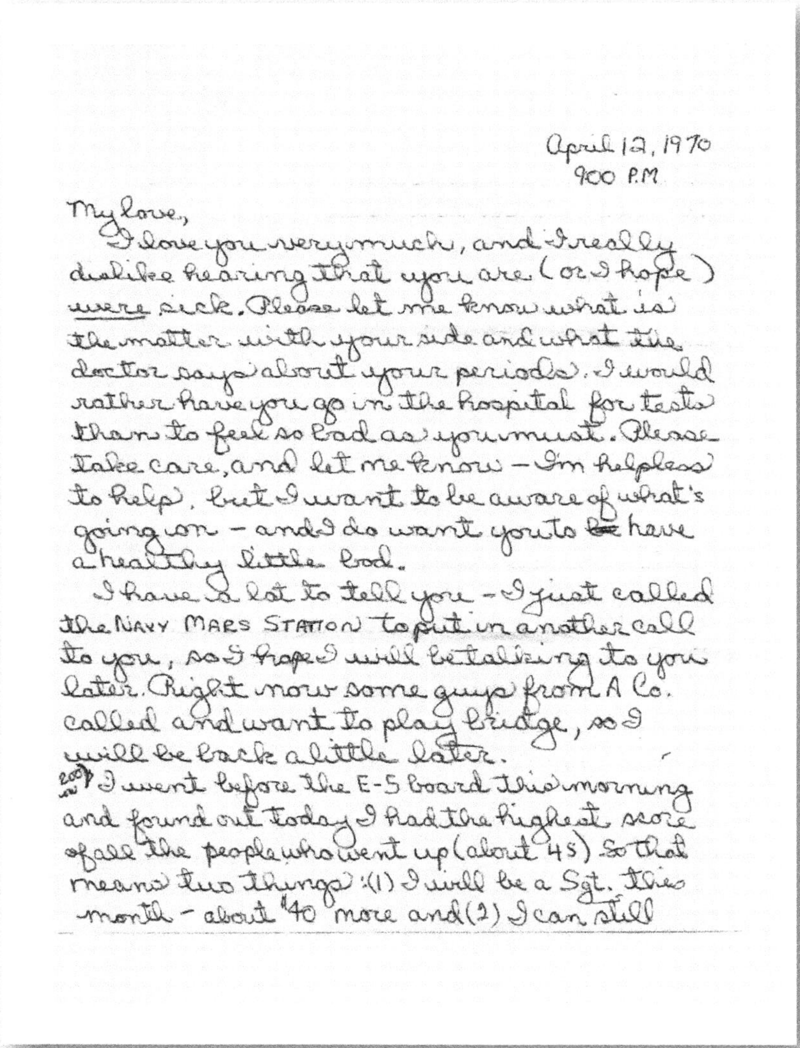

April 12, 1970
900 P.M

My love,

I love you very much, and I really dislike hearing that you are (or I hope) were sick. Please let me know what is the matter with your side and what the doctor says about your periods. I would rather have you go in the hospital for tests than to feel so bad as you must. Please take care, and let me know – I'm helpless to help, but I want to be aware of what's going on – and I do want you to ~~be~~ have a healthy little bod.

I have a lot to tell you – I just called the NAVY MARS STATION to put in another call to you, so I hope I will be talking to you later. Right now some guys from A Co. called and want to play bridge, so I will be back a little later.

200p I went before the E-5 board this morning and found out today I had the highest score of all the people who went up (about 45) So that means two things: (1) I will be a Sgt. this month – about $40 more and (2) I can still bullshit pretty well in interviews. I tried to be promoted into a Clerks MOS, but some regulation says you can't do it. Once an 11B always an 11B.

Earlier this evening I wrote a letter to Senator Percy thanking him for voting against Carswell. I would hated to have seen that man get it. I also asked him to stop the war in Vietnam – maybe he'll do it? —

I sent the money and the order in for your ring, your Mom's ring, and that necklace set for my Mom. They will all be mailed to you Air Mail, so you can get a card from us and send it to my Mom. Also I received the package a few days ago. I got the strap for my shades, candy bars, chips, sardines, sweat socks, and (I thought) a can of tennis balls. Tonight I was looking at it again and discovered they were handballs not tennis balls. Thank you. But, I didn't see any handball gloves in the box. Did you forget to send them or what?

Utah came back to the company three days ago. He had a job in Cam Ranh Bay for 30 days. I really feel sorry for him having to go back out to the field. I wish he could get a rear job.

Well love that's about it for now. It's about 1:15 and I must get some sleep. I just hope they can get the call through. Remember I love you very much.

Love
Bob

29 April 1970

Hi Love,

I got your letter about going to the doctor and running out of pills... Please go to a specialist and have him check you out. I think it is necessary, and also to find out about the pain in your side. Keep me informed.

Some days - in fact a lot of days - are like today. Not good and not too bad - sort of blah. I'll give you a quick rundown:

Worked last night till midnight on two court martials.
Got up at 6:45 this morning
Took all my paperwork to Bn. Hdqtrs.
Came back and ate breakfast.
Finished typing 4 witness statements for C.M.
Filled out R and R forms for about 35 people.
Typed out papers for 5 guys promotion to E4
Ate lunch
Answered a million questions after lunch about stupid paperwork and requests for leave, reassign., etc.
Typed out clearance papers for 2 guys going home.
Typed out a request for reassignment

Figured out foxhole report and called it
in - how many people in field
Figured out status report and typed it
out - where everyone in Co. is located
Ate dinner (Ice cream and milk)
Played tennis - didn't really enjoy it
(played doubles - that's probably
why I'm sorta blah)
Played bridge till 9:00 (no good hands)
Typed out Morning Report
It's now 11:15.

I need to get away from this place
for awhile, a change of scenery or
something. I wish it were June 29
instead of April. Well, I'm down to
about 80 days now and getting
shorter. You can see by my run down of
the days, that I'm just biding my
time, and sometimes like tonight
dissatisfied that I don't try to do more
constructive things like read.

I would like for you to look into
something for me please. I read some-
where that as a Vietnam veteran I
am eligible to get some sort of money
from the State of Illinois. Maybe you
could find out by calling the Army

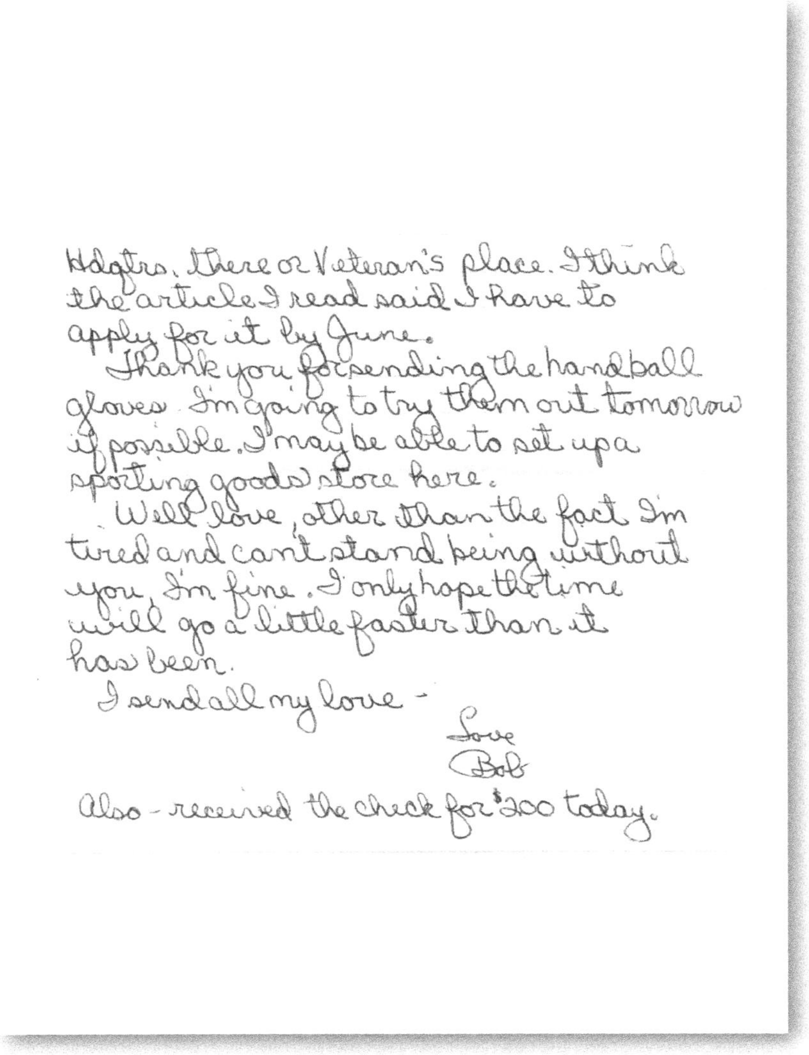

Hdqtrs. there or Veteran's place. I think the article I read said I have to apply for it by June.

Thank you for sending the handball gloves. I'm going to try them out tomorrow if possible. I may be able to set up a sporting goods store here.

Well love, other than the fact I'm tired and can't stand being without you, I'm fine. I only hope the time will go a little faster than it has been.

I send all my love -

Love
Bob

Also - received the check for $200 today.

24 June 70

Hi Love,

Well it finally came. I haven't seen the orders yet so I don't know whether I will get any drop, but we know where we will live! Kansas. Yep right in the heart of the Great Plains States. Well I can't say that I'm real happy about it, but I don't really care that much - we'll be together AT LAST! It is Fort Riley, Kansas and looks like it is fairly close to Manhattan, Ks (Ks State University) I'll send you a copy of the orders when I get them and let you know about the drop. If I had to guess I would say I'll probably be in the States about the 19th. I will have to report about the 25th of August to Ft. Riley (I mean we will)

Should I write to Mary and Gary or do you want to call? I think anytime after the 4th or 5th of August would be fine. That way we can

spend some time alone in Chicago
and then to Decatur, maybe Bloomington and Nashville. I'd like to
get out to see Doug and Meg but
I kind of doubt we can be
trāpsing all over the country.
Let me know what Gary says or if
you want me to write. We could
Read West from Nashville and
spend the rest of the time there.
I had the Red Cross here contact
the Decatur Red Cross to find
out about Dad. It only took about
20 hours to get a reply. Dr. Spicer
said that Dad was doing as
well as could be expected, but
that it wasn't necessary for me
to be there. Of course I'm glad to
hear that he is a little better
b.it I was hoping the doctor
might be a little more helpful
in getting me back early. I
know how much he appreciates
your help and concern, so just
keep doing what you can. I know
you will without my advice but

I just want you to know that I appreciate it also. I guess that's just one of the thousand reasons I married you.

About the loan - yes it is correct, so go ahead and send the check.

No more news except that we're down to 26 DAYS AND COUNTING. It won't be long my love so keep the faith a little more.

All my love,

Bob

28 June

Hello you beautiful doll,

You want to know what I'm doing the rest of my life? I'll tell you this - you won't be wondering much longer. You'll know, because whatever I'm doing you'll be doing it too.

I am really anxious to see the stereo equipment. From the way you described it, it must be outstanding. Have you tried it out? I am getting a cartridge (and diamond needle) from Hong Kong. I'll bring that with me. You can get them there for $20 and there about $50 - $60 in the States. I should also be getting the camera I ordered very soon. But I'll just hang on to that rather than sending it back.

I'm sending you a couple of copies of my orders. On the 17th I sign out of the company and the division. Then I'll fly to

Cam Ranh Bay on the 18th and probably leave there the 20th. or sooner if I can!! Only 22 MORE DAYS!!

I checked out Ft. Riley and it's about 475 from Rock Island. It's also 475 East of Denver, 500 miles North of Dallas and 275 mi South of Des Moines. ~~So that~~ will be our new home. I will write now and try to get some information on housing, and have it sent to you.

I will cut this short since it is the middle of the afternoon. I love you and - Oh yes - I did receive the 2 packages and the butterscotch brownies were O.K. The crunchy stuff with a jelly filling was outstanding.

All my love,

Bob

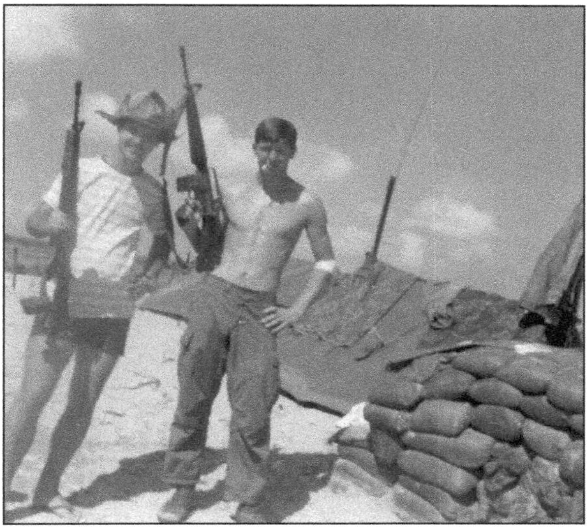

Utah and me a few weeks after arriving in country at a camp fortified with sand bunkers set up close to the South China sea.

I am pictured with our fifteen-year old interpreter, Bo, who spoke English well and helped us interrogate suspected enemies. Most every company employed one of these young kids.

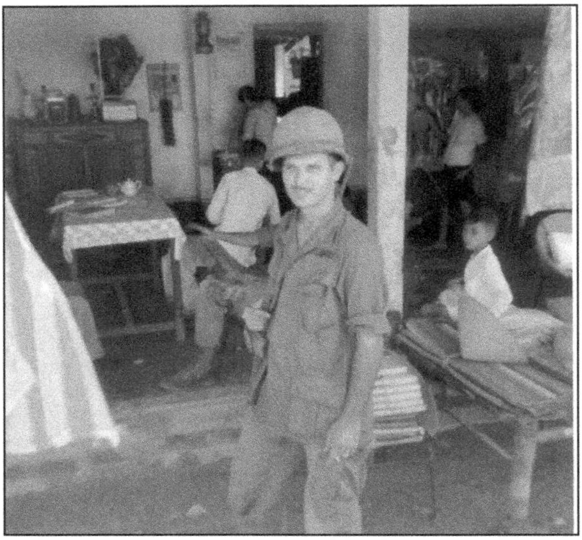

I am in one of the villages that surrounded our Landing Zone. Villages in the field where most rice paddy farmers lived did not have stands (like in this picture) set up to sell things.

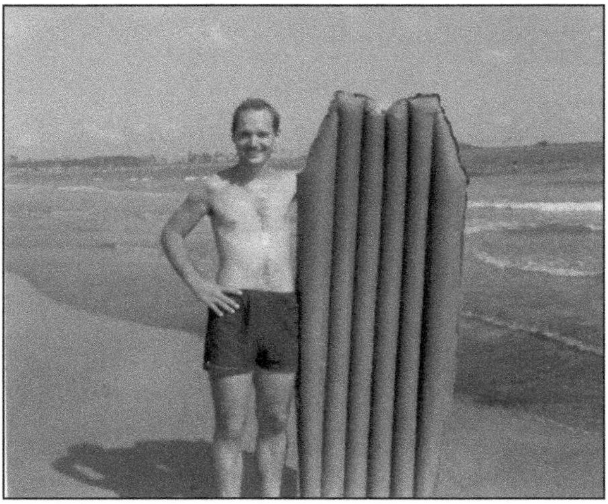

I only remember one time in the field when we stayed on the beach at the South China Sea. It was a luxury for us because it was easy to secure the area and we even got to use inflatable mattresses to go in the water.

The rear area Bravo Company sign at LZ Gator our headquarters. The LZ was safer than the field but suffered one attack during my time in Vietnam when we killed five enemy soldiers.

A picture with seven of our guys. In front is Wally Gator (from Chicago) and Bob Van Zandt (from Detroit). In back are Tanner (who was the machine gunner), Doc (our medic), big Cal, Me and Utah.

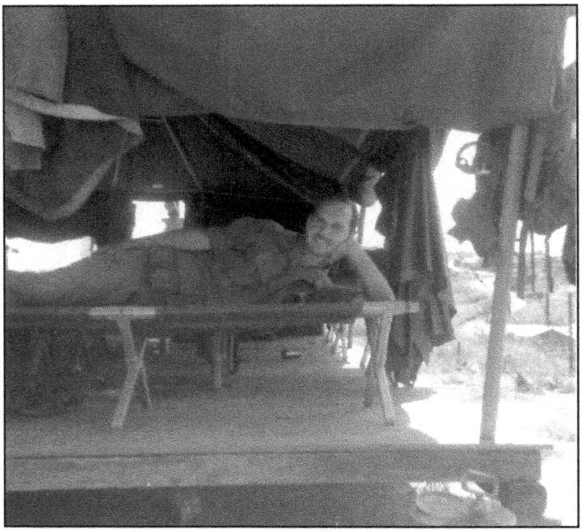

This was my cot that I slept on when we were at LZ Gator (unless I was on guard duty).

I am reading one of Connie's many letters she sent that were always an encouragement to me. Notice dog tags on my neck and my M-16 rifle by my side.

Two guys from our platoon—Ray Masecchia and Leslie Van Bieber our platoon sergeant (the one who never took off his socks in the field!)

Picture of me in the rear area the first time we returned from the field at the end of August.

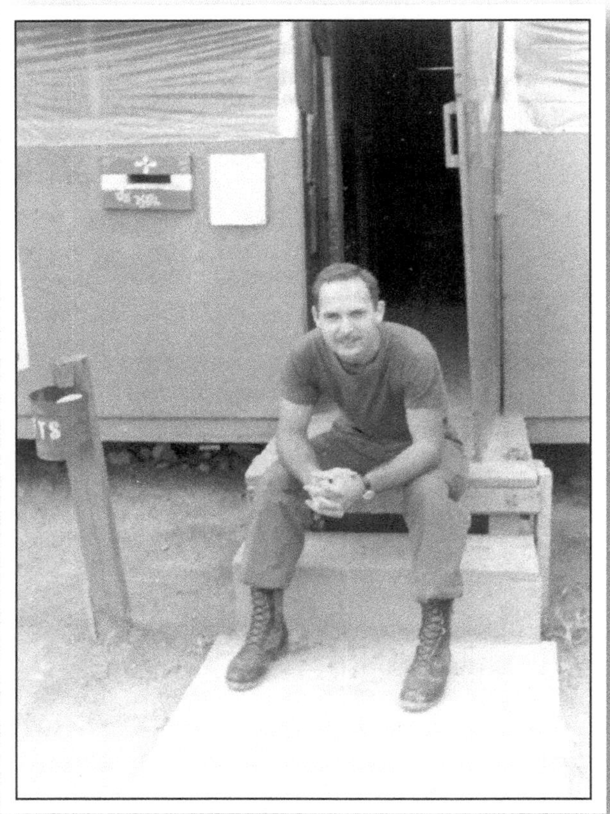

I'm sitting on the steps of the headquarters for our company. I worked inside this building with the mail clerk until early March when we moved the headquarters into Chu Lai.

This fuzzy picture of me and my friend Lt. Larry Betts, taken at LZ Gator, is the only remaining photo I have of the two of us.

Larry Betts' wife of only a few months, Diana, and Larry Jr., a son that Larry never met. Diana found out she was pregnant the same day she found out Larry had been killed in Vietnam.

Breakfast with Diana and her husband, Norm. Larry Jr. and Melissa brought their children, Larry III, and Maddie, who wanted to hear about their grandfather Betts who fought in the Vietnam War with me.

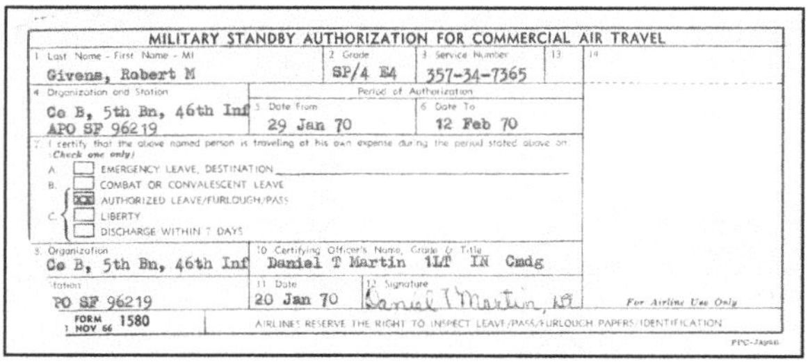

MILITARY STANDBY AUTHORIZATION FOR COMMERCIAL AIR TRAVEL

1 Last Name - First Name - MI: Givens, Robert M
2 Grade: SP/4 E4
3 Service Number: 357-34-7365
13
14

4 Organization and Station: Co B, 5th Bn, 46th Inf APO SF 96219

Period of Authorization
5 Date From: 29 Jan 70
6 Date To: 12 Feb 70

7 I certify that the above named person is traveling at his own expense during the period stated above on: (Check one only)
A. [ ] EMERGENCY LEAVE, DESTINATION ____
B. [ ] COMBAT OR CONVALESCENT LEAVE
C. [X] AUTHORIZED LEAVE/FURLOUGH/PASS
[ ] LIBERTY
[ ] DISCHARGE WITHIN 7 DAYS

8 Organization: Co B, 5th Bn, 46th Inf
Station: PO SF 96219
10 Certifying Officer's Name, Grade & Title: Daniel T Martin 1LT IN Cmdg
11 Date: 20 Jan 70
12 Signature: Daniel T Martin

For Airline Use Only

FORM 1 NOV 66 1580

AIRLINES RESERVE THE RIGHT TO INSPECT LEAVE/PASS/FURLOUGH PAPERS/IDENTIFICATION

PPC-Japan

Military standby orders that Connie used to fly on a low-cost fare to Hawaii.

They Are Bound For Hawaii

Reading travel folders on Hawaii are three members of the Waiting Wives club who are planning upcoming R and R vacations in that state with their husbands. From left, are Mrs. Tom Zelni, Moline; Mrs. Manny Ruscheinski, East Moline; and Mrs. Robert Givens, Rock Island. The next meeting of the Waiting Wives Club is at 8 p.m. Saturday, Jan. 31, in the Caisson Room, Rock Island Arsenal cafeteria building. Women with husbands or fiances in the service are invited to attend. R and R is service lingo for rest and recreation.

Rock Island newspaper article about Connie and two other military wives bound for Hawaii to meet their husbands.

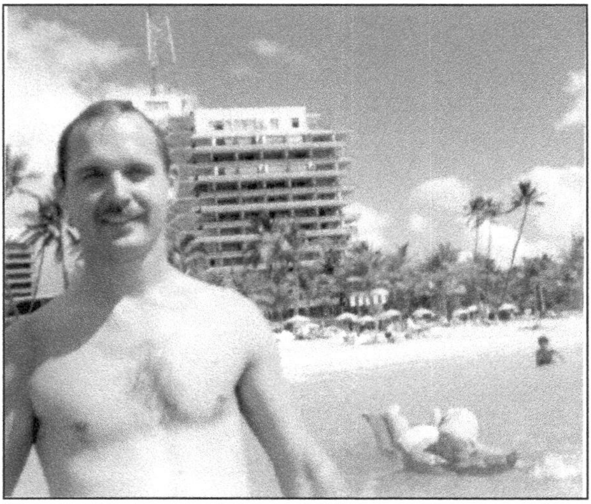

Swimming in the beautiful waters of Waikiki Beach with our upscale hotel in the background.

Selfie on Waikiki Beach.

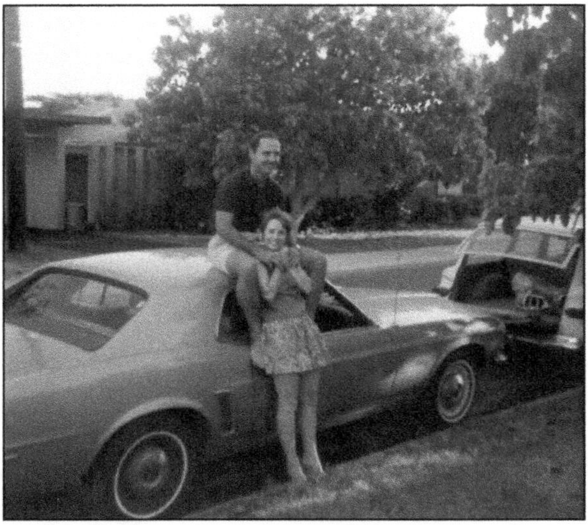

We enjoyed driving around the island with this Mustang rental car. I had not driven any vehicle since the summer.

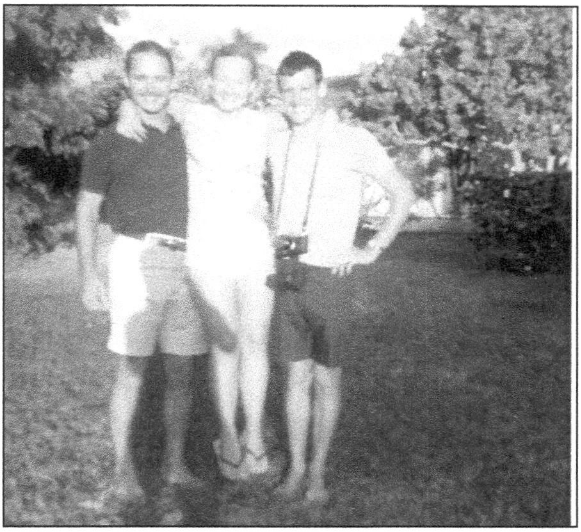

Enjoying time with our college friends Bob and Cindy Deffenbaugh. Bob was stationed at Pearl Harbor, Hawaii.

Fore! Connie is attempting a trick shot (at my expense). No damage was done to my mouth.

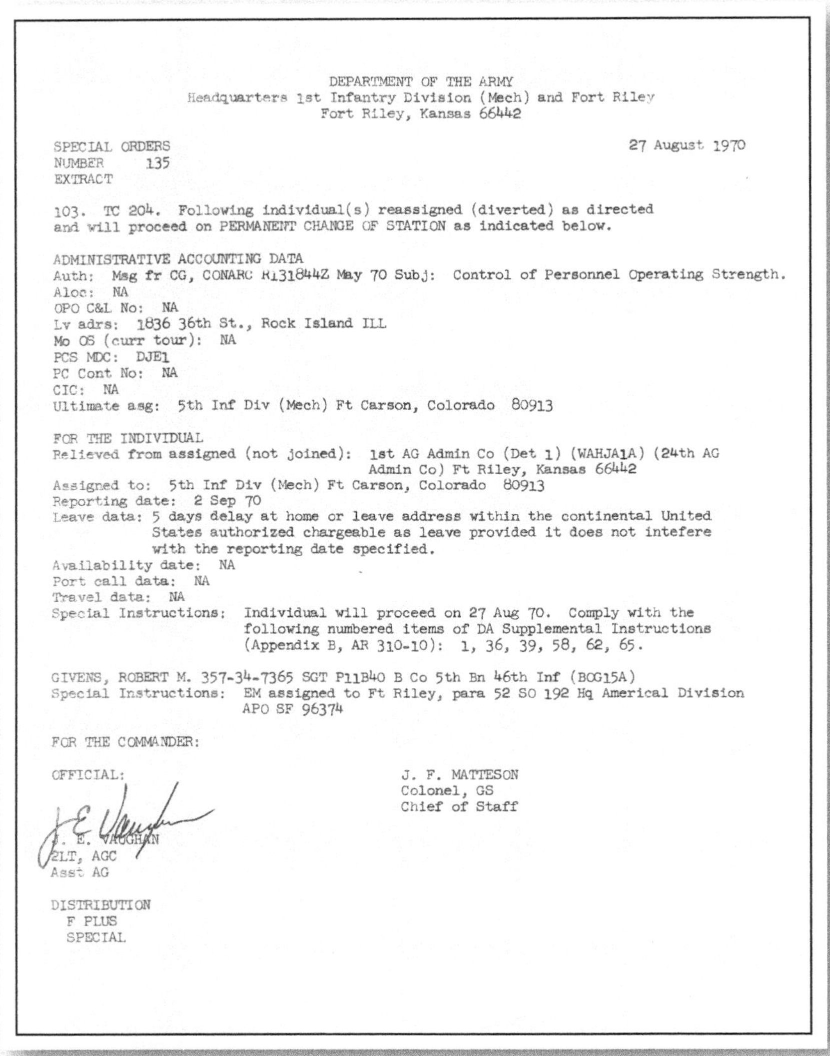

DEPARTMENT OF THE ARMY
Headquarters 1st Infantry Division (Mech) and Fort Riley
Fort Riley, Kansas 66442

SPECIAL ORDERS
NUMBER 135
EXTRACT

27 August 1970

103. TC 204. Following individual(s) reassigned (diverted) as directed and will proceed on PERMANENT CHANGE OF STATION as indicated below.

ADMINISTRATIVE ACCOUNTING DATA
Auth: Msg fr CG, CONARC R131844Z May 70 Subj: Control of Personnel Operating Strength.
Aloc: NA
OPO C&L No: NA
Lv adrs: 1836 36th St., Rock Island ILL
Mo OS (curr tour): NA
PCS MDC: DJE1
PC Cont No: NA
CIC: NA
Ultimate asg: 5th Inf Div (Mech) Ft Carson, Colorado 80913

FOR THE INDIVIDUAL
Relieved from assigned (not joined): 1st AG Admin Co (Det 1) (WAHJA1A) (24th AG Admin Co) Ft Riley, Kansas 66442
Assigned to: 5th Inf Div (Mech) Ft Carson, Colorado 80913
Reporting date: 2 Sep 70
Leave data: 5 days delay at home or leave address within the continental United States authorized chargeable as leave provided it does not intefere with the reporting date specified.
Availability date: NA
Port call data: NA
Travel data: NA
Special Instructions: Individual will proceed on 27 Aug 70. Comply with the following numbered items of DA Supplemental Instructions (Appendix B, AR 310-10): 1, 36, 39, 58, 62, 65.

GIVENS, ROBERT M. 357-34-7365 SGT P11B40 B Co 5th Bn 46th Inf (BCG15A)
Special Instructions: EM assigned to Ft Riley, para 52 SO 192 Hq Americal Division APO SF 96374

FOR THE COMMANDER:

OFFICIAL:

J. E. VAUGHAN
2LT, AGC
Asst AG

J. F. MATTESON
Colonel, GS
Chief of Staff

DISTRIBUTION
F PLUS
SPECIAL

Our original orders were for Fort Riley in Junction City, Kansas. New orders were cut for us to go to a much nicer locale—Fort Carson in Colorado Springs.

SIX

WELCOME HOME SOLDIER

"THANK YOU FOR YOUR SERVICE"

Returning soldiers were aware of the war at home and the mass protests taking place on the streets of our cities and on college campuses. We all had heard the reports about the angry mobs congregated around military bases and how violent anti-war demonstrations had progressively escalated throughout the States. We'd also heard about the horrible shootings at Kent State University and the massive demonstrations that resulted. But returning soldiers had no real idea what kind of hostile, inflammatory environment they might personally encounter upon their return. Would they be defiantly confronted and questioned? Probably. Would they be verbally and even physically harassed? Maybe. Would they be indiscriminately called out as murderers or baby killers? Perhaps. They only were certain of one thing—they would not be warmly welcomed home like heroes as were soldiers from World War I or World War II—nor did they expect such a welcome. In truth, the likelihood for these Vietnam veterans was that they would not be welcomed home by anyone except their closest relatives, and even that positive reception was not a sure thing.

Marine Lt. and author Karl Marlantes describes an incident that happened to him upon his return from Vietnam:

> I boarded a train for New York at Union Station [Washington D.C.]. I was in uniform, even though we had explicit instructions to avoid problems by not wearing our uniforms around civilians. This put us in a bit of a bind. You could get half price tickets on trains and air fare going standby, but only if you were in uniform ....
>
> I passed a nice-looking woman who looked up at me and quickly looked away ... I found a seat at the far end of the car and settled down to read but wished I were talking to her instead. About five minutes later I saw her get up and come down the aisle. She was looking right at me, lips pressed tight. She stood in front of me and spit on me. I was trembling with shame and embarrassment .... People hid behind their newspapers. Some looked intently out dark windows.
>
> I wiped the spit off as best I could and pretended to go back to reading, trying to control the shaking. The woman moved to another car. Small victory. I eventually moved to a different car in the opposite direction, embarrassed to stay where people had seen what happened.[1]

These repulsive displays of anger and disrespect toward soldiers are hard to imagine in today's world where soldiers are generally respected, even honored, for their service to their country. But in 1970 it happened, just not to everyone. I don't know how I would have reacted if someone spit on me. I'm pretty sure I at least would have lashed out verbally if not physically. Fortunately for me, I never had to make that choice. Some others did. The times were different.

Gold Star mothers, those who lost a son in the war, were often maligned by anti-war protesters. Emogene Cupp, National President, recalled that society's ill treatment of veterans extended even to their families. "It was very hurtful," she recalled. "They treated the moms the same way as they treated the vets. They weren't nice. They either ignored you and wished you would go away or people would ask, 'Why did you let them go?'" Imagine that! Her only son Robert, an Army draftee, was killed by a land mine on his twenty-first birthday, June 6, 1968.[2]

John Kerry, the future senator from Massachusetts and 2004 US Presidential candidate, tells a story about falling asleep on a flight going from San Francisco to New York. He woke up startled and yelling from some wartime flashback. Passengers physically moved away from him. Kerry said: "This country doesn't give a [crap} about the guys coming back or what they'd gone through. The feeling toward them was, stay away—don't contaminate us with whatever you've brought back from Vietnam. This type of reaction made many veterans feel alone and isolated from the rest of American society."[3]

What the soldier quickly understood as he tried to blend back into civilian life was the troubling fact that most people did not make any distinction between the war and the warrior. Their attitude was that they hated the war and, ipso facto, they also despised the soldier who was fighting in it. For whatever reasons, they could not separate the two. It would take many years, a memorial wall, and an empathetic US president before that separation of soldier and war became a significant reality.

The transition from living the life of a combat soldier in a war zone to a veteran stationed at a sterile, safe US military base was shockingly sudden and starkly different—from sleeping each night on the ground in enemy territory, eating tasteless C-rations out of a can every day, using nature to relieve yourself (or the "luxury" of an outhouse if you were in a rear area), setting up smoke grenades at night to alert you to enemy attackers, guarding against enemy guerilla attacks, frequently being under fire from enemy small-arms fire, carefully avoiding trip wires or mines as you humped along the trails, constantly protecting each other but still seeing your comrades get wounded or killed. One day the soldier is in mortal danger in Vietnam; less than twenty-four hours later he is safely on U.S. soil. There was no grace period or de-briefing time for recalibration for these soldiers. In other wars, soldiers returned home with their buddies from their units over a period of weeks at sea. This time together allowed for some communal camaraderie and an informal de-briefing of sorts.

There was no such grace period for the Vietnam veteran who likely didn't know one person on his returning flight. One day in Vietnam, the next day in Decatur, Illinois. Go figure it out, soldier. Just don't expect any warm reception or gratitude. Even friends didn't know what to say if the topic of Vietnam came up; there often was just a furtive glance and an awkward silence. No one, *no one*, ever said, "Thank you for your service," to a returning veteran in 1970.

I Can Almost Touch Freedom

About a week before I was scheduled to return home from Vietnam, the Red Cross contacted my infantry unit in Chu Lai and told them that Sergeant Givens' father was hospitalized in Decatur, Illinois, after a severe heart attack. My dad was not expected to survive; they recommended that I be given emergency leave to return to the United States. The military was generally lenient and surprisingly efficient in these kinds of family emergency situations. Within twenty hours of being notified, I departed Vietnam and landed at Sea-Tac Airport in Seattle, Washington. Here is the story of how I was notified of the situation and of my emergency leave.

My tour of duty in Vietnam would be over on July 21, and by the first week in July my replacement for the company clerk job, Bob Yantzie, was sent back to our headquarters so I could train him on the job. Since I had little work to do after the training was completed (he actually knew how to type!), the Executive Officer (XO) assigned me to take an American prisoner from our small facility in Chu Lai to the Long Binh Jail, the largest American prison facility very close to Saigon. So, on July 12, I flew on a military cargo plane to deliver my prisoner to Long Binh. I had no specific orders on when to return, so I decided to spend the next day, July 13, in the Long Binh/Saigon area since I had never seen South Vietnam's largest city.

Little did I realize that the American Red Cross was frantically searching for me. The Red Cross in the United States had made contact with Connie. They notified her on July 13 that I was on some special assignment in the Long Binh area, and they had not yet been able to locate me. They would keep trying and let her know once I was on my way home. They advised her that if she wanted to see her father-in-law alive, she should get to Decatur, Illinois, right away. He wasn't expected to live through the night. Connie immediately drove three hours from Rock Island to Decatur to see my dad in the hospital.

Meanwhile, after spending one day in Saigon, I got on an early-morning cargo flight on July 14, heading back up north to Chu Lai. My presence on the flight was relayed to our company. The moment I disembarked the plane, I was given a jeep ride to our company area and told to see the chaplain, the medical doctor, pack up, and prepare to leave country immediately. I didn't have time to pack some things that under a less time-constrained situation I would have brought home. Those things included all of the letters that Connie had written to me while I was in Vietnam. She had saved all of my letters, but, unfortunately, her letters were left behind and eventually discarded. By early afternoon I was on a flight back to Saigon to get on a plane that night for the United States.

As I waited at the Saigon Airport to board a flight for the States, my head was literally swimming with emotion from the frenetic events of the day. Everything seemed to be operating in accelerated mode even as I tried to calm myself, think clearly, and act normally. I waited anxiously with three other soldiers to see if I would be able to board the last plane of the evening leaving for the United States. These two soldiers, also on emergency leave, said they heard that the plane was full, and we might not leave until the next day. At this point my emotions were frazzled, so that comment was not particularly helpful. Now that I was this close to leaving Vietnam, I desperately wanted out—from the dangers that surrounded me in this country, from the constant sounds of war and putrid smells I knew from almost twelve months in this environment, and from a living and working existence where I had little or no control over any aspect of my life. Because I was so close to escaping this war zone, and even though I was in a reasonably safe and heavily guarded military airport, I had trouble dismissing thoughts of something bad happening at this late stage of my tour of duty. I desperately thought, "Get me out of here. I can almost touch freedom."

Leaving Vietnam

"Sergeant Givens," I heard a sharp voice call out. "Get ready to board this flight that is now on the tarmac." The person called out the names of the other two men who were also waiting to go home on emergency leave. I watched as three men who had been on the plane were escorted back to the waiting area. These three were forced to give up their seats for the three of us on emergency leave. I am so glad that I never came face to face with these three soldiers who must have been emotionally crushed to be minutes from departing and then involuntarily removed from the plane. Can you imagine their angst and disappointment?

The three of us on emergency leave were ushered onto the plane and given seats close to the front. I sat down, closed my eyes, and wondered "Is this really the end of my tour in Vietnam? Am I really going home?" As the time for their tour of duty drew short (meaning less than sixty days left in country), every soldier had a calendar where they marked off the approaching days and circled their return date. Only eight hours earlier, I had returned from an assignment in Long Binh thinking I still had another seven days in this country. Sitting with great anticipation on this plane headed to freedom, I didn't dare open my eyes. Without saying a word to anyone, I pleaded silently to a God I did not yet know, "Please let this plane take off, please take off." I did not open my eyes until the plane, only a few minutes later, began to taxi and then laboriously lift off the ground. I noticed the friendly face of the flight attendant looking my way. She smiled at me in a manner that communicated she understood my emotional drama. She later explained to me the drill—soldiers were boisterous on the way over, silent on the return. Unbelievable I thought. It's over. I really am on my way home!

I knew the situation with my dad was serious, but my thoughts were mostly that I was returning home to my beloved wife. I fought the tears. For me, there was great anticipation and hope. I was returning to a person who loved me with all her heart and soul and was waiting for me with open arms. So many of the returning men did not have such a care giver/ soul mate waiting for them. They were walking into firestorms they did not expect and were ill prepared for—including people who thought they were stupid for going to Vietnam and, even worse, who took pleasure in verbally berating and abusing them. Some experienced protesters brazenly shouting obscenities at them and calling them murderers and baby killers. Why were they blaming and accusing us? No wonder Vietnam veterans rarely spoke about their war experiences with other people.

The only people to ever hear me talk in any detail about my war experiences were, first, my wife and then, much later, my children. Connie and I always had been open with each other. We fully trusted one another and wanted to know our feelings about the significant events in our lives, and, of course, Vietnam was significant for both of us. It helped me when I returned to have someone to process things with, and it helped her to better understand my reactions to certain events and situations. For example, I overreacted to sudden loud noises that made me slightly defensive and uneasy. There were times at night when I would awaken from a nightmare with a yell. Connie would touch me gently to reassure me that everything was OK and that I was safe. Also, even before Vietnam I always liked being in control. Circumstances where I had little or no control were often uncomfortable for me, and my time in Vietnam was an example. I did not want to repeat that experience as a civilian.

Over time I related my Vietnam experiences to Connie, always an empathetic listener, without some of the gruesome details. Describing those same events in any detail to others, even friends, seemed fruitless. How could I describe Vietnam experiences objectively so others might understand and do so without making it seem like someone trying to act like a tough guy or some kind of embattled warrior? I learned a valuable lesson from my war-time experiences—I endured things in Vietnam that I might never have thought possible. Even so, I wasn't that special. Most anyone else in similar circumstances could have done the same thing. It's just that few would *choose* to endure those hardships. Painting an accurate picture to others with the right personal perspective wasn't easy then and is not easy now. So, most of us, myself included, just remained relatively quiet about our efforts in the war.

Finally, Home to Connie

When we landed in Seattle on the morning of July 15, all personnel were ordered to stay seated while the three men on emergency leave were escorted off the plane. There was a separate clearance facility for those on emergency leave; we processed back to the States in less than fifteen minutes. The procedure usually took many hours for everyone else returning on normal status. Less than two hours after landing in Seattle, I was on a non-stop flight to Chicago all arranged by the Red Cross working together with the Army. If there were anti-war protesters in the Seattle Airport (as I'm sure there were), I was too focused on getting to my next flight to notice them. Connie's brother, Dale Richeson, himself a Vietnam veteran, met me at O'Hare Airport and drove me to Decatur where Connie was waiting for me at the house where Dad lived.

We embraced and kissed as our eyes were filled with tears. I asked Connie if Dad was still alive. She said yes, and he is waiting for you. How prophetic those words proved to be! I stepped into Dad's room at the hospital not knowing what to expect or even if he was alert enough to speak with me. His eyes were wide open as I approached his bed and he had a warm smile on his face. I bent down and gave him a gentle but loving hug. He kissed me on the cheek. We talked for fifteen minutes. He was lucid and interested in everything I had to say. Then when the nurse said it was time for me to leave, he asked me one important question: "Bob," he inquired, "do you have to return to Vietnam?" "No, Dad, I'm home to stay," I told him proudly. "Good," he said with his eyes sparkling at me. I left the hospital room late that afternoon; about two hours later the doctor (a personal friend of Dad's) phoned and said your father just passed away. Dad held on and waited to die until he was sure I was home safely from overseas. I love you, Dad.

The funeral was attended by most of the Givens side of the family from Chicago, and my cousin Ralph Shankland (Dad's nephew) and his wife from California. Ralph was a Korean war veteran who loved and respected my dad. Dad had given him a job when he returned from the war and helped him get back on his feet financially. Some of these relatives were people who had helped me (and my Mom) when we desperately needed financial assistance. Among those were my lawyer cousin from Chicago, Norm Schmitz and his wife Mary Jane. I worked three jobs during college to pay for college expenses and to pay bills at home including our monthly rent. Norm and Mary Jane's generosity was as encouraging to me as it was necessary. I graduated Millikin with very little debt. These relatives remembered Dad in the best and fondest ways, and I loved them for their gracious, caring attitude and for their genuine support. Dad died on his 70th birthday, July 15, 1970. I was comforted by the fact that he lived long enough to welcome me home and that he died peacefully. The services at the funeral home and at Graceland Cemetery in Decatur were dignified and solemn. But even though Dad had struggled physically over the last fifteen years of his life, I thought seventy represented a long and very old age (at age seventy-five, I think a bit differently today.)

My brother, Charles, and I split the costs for the funeral. Mr. Moran (the funeral home owner) was a friend of Dad's. He took a minimum down payment from us, and let us pay as we were able over the next four years. I generally made monthly payments to the funeral home. I don't know whether my brother ever paid his fair share of the bill, but Mr. Moran was generous to us and we never received any statements or demands for payment. A lot of people loved my father.

Connie and I left Decatur after the funeral and drove to Nashville to see my mother. We got a motel room close by her one-bedroom apartment and intended to stay four or five days. My mother was not very mobile physically and could not drive, so she depended on other people to help her even with mundane daily tasks like making coffee, grocery shopping, or bringing her a meal. I truly was happy to see my mother, and she lovingly welcomed me home and was glad I was finally safe. But rather quickly that welcome turned into a tedious drudgery of menial and time-consuming tasks to provide for my mother's needs. I hit my limit overload when she gave me a bundle of clothes to take to the local do-it-yourself laundromat. This job gave me awful flashbacks to times growing up when we did not own a working washer or dryer. Almost once a week I was required to carry several laundry bags of clothes five or six blocks to a local laundromat. Two hours later I would walk home with clean clothes in tow. Early on day three as we were finishing the last load of clothes for Mom in Nashville, Connie was surprised (but not shocked) when I said, "We're dropping these clothes off to Mom and then leaving." I was home now, and it would be three more weeks before we had to report to my new assignment at Fort Riley, Kansas. I just wanted to make my own decisions and not have someone (including my mother) order me around. With the time spent at the funeral and time in Nashville, I was ready to spend alone time with Connie and then maybe see a few close friends. Connie fully understood that this laundry detail was too much; it was the final straw for me with Mom for this visit. Eight years later Mom came to live with us because of declining health and we, particularly Connie, would look after and serve her on a daily basis. But now was not that time. We dropped off Mom's clean clothes at her apartment, I gave her a hug and a kiss, and informed her we were leaving immediately to drive back to Illinois. Honestly my independence was important to me; I couldn't get out of Nashville fast enough.

We did make time to spend a long weekend with our college friends the Deffenbaugh's in Western Michigan. We had seen Bob and Cindy six months earlier in Hawaii. Cindy's parents owned a nice home on Lake Michigan and we enjoyed a fun time with them boating, swimming, and playing yard games.

When we reported for duty in late August at Fort Riley, Kansas, I was in for a big surprise. First of all, the temperature was a boiling hot 110°. We had rented an apartment in Junction City, and our small amount of furniture was in transit. I pulled up to the reporting station while Connie remained in the car. When the clerk could not find my orders, he asked my rank. I told him Sgt. E-5. "Oh yes," he responded. "There's a special file here for Infantry E-5s. Here's your name. Your orders are for Germany." "What!", I shouted in shock. "Impossible." I was incredulous. Just at that moment the Captain in charge walked by and I literally reached out and grabbed his arm. "Sir," I exclaimed, "I just returned from Vietnam, I only have six months left in the service, my wife is waiting in the car, and our furniture is on the way here, I can't go to Germany." Somehow my plea seemed to get through to him. After briefly looking me over (I was in civilian clothes) he asked, "What's your name?" "Sgt. Givens, sir." "OK Sgt.," he responded, "Report here at 0800 hours tomorrow to get your orders." I looked a bit shell-shocked when I got to the car and told Connie what had just happened. The next morning I picked up my orders to report to Fort Carson in Colorado Springs, Colorado. Hallelujah! We had gone to Colorado Springs for our honeymoon just two years prior. Thank you, Captain.

Hate the War. Hate the Soldier

I had significant re-entry advantages over the typical returning soldier. I was twenty-five years old and married with a Master's Degree in Higher Education. By the time I was drafted, I had finished six years of college and started my career. The university where I was employed was required by law to hire me back (if I so chose) in the same or a similar position. Also, I was healthy. I had sustained no physical injuries or long-term emotional scars. My wife of twenty-three months was an established elementary school teacher. Connie sent me three letters a week and two boxes of books, food, and snacks twice a month for one year. She faithfully counted down the days with me until I would return home. We even were able to spend one week together in Hawaii in February, 1970. Most returning soldiers did not have this kind of support and encouragement during their tour of duty or when they returned home.

The average age of soldiers serving in the infantry in Vietnam was around nineteen to twenty—kids really. Many of these boys came of age in Vietnam. They often did not have the advantage of a four-year college degree, an established career path, a loving wife, and perhaps any kind of stable home environment. Some, like Bob Van Zandt a bright eighteen-year-old kid in our infantry company from Detroit, were given the choice of jail, generally for non-violent offenses like robbery (not a particularly bright move for an intelligent kid), or, alternatively, joining the Army. Bob, like most others, chose the Army. Many of these men were so young that they had no experience living an independent life—developing and supporting a family, looking for a job and starting a career, or even saving money. Therefore, it should be no great surprise that these young veterans returning from Vietnam had trouble adjusting to some sort of a routine, stable life in the States. Our government was not always helpful. The Army in those days did not recognize certain physical and mental by-products of the war, like PTSD (Post Traumatic Stress Disorder) and diseases from Agent Orange exposure, the toxic defoliant used in Vietnam that affected many soldiers. Veterans hospitals and clinics were not funded well enough to serve the needs of so many returning soldiers.

In addition, the psychological ailments could be worse than the physical ones. As recounted in these pages, veterans had to deal with people eager to berate them for serving in the military in what these individuals considered an immoral and ignoble cause; some were in-your-face-screamers and way over the line in terms of distasteful and occasionally abhorrent behavior. The stories are rampant in books and magazines about this era.

But perhaps more subtle and more insidious, and certainly more personally and deeply damaging, was the pervasive, scathing undertone of our country at the time. Most civilians, whether for or against the war, made no distinction between the actions of the government that had started the war, forcing these young men to serve, and the returning soldiers themselves who had just given two years of their lives to the country. These soldiers were not close to being recognized as returning heroes or even just dutiful soldiers serving their country. For sure, that kind of recognition was not of utmost importance to most returning veterans who didn't need or expect any special welcome home. They wanted just a modicum of respect, they wanted to get on with their lives, and they wanted to be left alone. For a number of people who were against the war and never served in it, these soldiers were categorized as immoral and even villains. And while not everyone felt or acted that way, those that did were often the vocal ones determined to make their strong, negative opinions known.

Returning veterans learned that the attitude and tone—the aura of our country—could be belittling and hurtful even without words or actions. These veterans were seldom recognized as honorable soldiers who had given of their time and risked their lives to serve their country.

How sad. The prevailing attitude in 1970 greeting veterans returning from Vietnam was how could you let yourself be drafted into this messy war? Were you some wide-eyed patriot or were you just plain stupid? (By the way, as this book describes, there are other alternative answers to that question.) What a dramatic change from people's attitudes about other war veterans. A hero? No way! Someone who deserves credit for serving their country for two years? You gotta be kidding. Welcome home, soldier!

— SEVEN —

A Hunger for Healing

The Forgotten Soldier

By the late 1980s, fifteen years after the last American troops surreptitiously and ignominiously exited Vietnam, the hostile anti-war demonstrations in our country had long stopped. Vietnam was rarely referenced or talked about in general or even in historical discussions. It was as if somehow that chapter of history had been ripped from the book and tossed aside ... or even totally ignored. World War I, World War II, and the Korean War were easy to talk about and celebrate, but Vietnam was still taboo. Questions surrounding our involvement in the Vietnam War were still complicated and unresolved. It was easier to tuck those issues away into an obscure corner rather than re-examine them. The prevailing attitude was that "We've gotten past this nasty period in our country's history, so let's just move on." Compared to other wars, the number of books written about soldiers' experiences in Vietnam, even to this day, is surprisingly limited in number and scope. Our nation indeed had moved on to other timelier issues, like American civilian hostages in the Middle East, an escalating cold war with Russia, and the continuing effects of racial strife. The Vietnam War was behind us and out of mind—as was the Vietnam veteran—largely forgotten, institutionally marginalized, without recognition, without honor.

Rarely did anyone except another Vietnam veteran ever asked me about Vietnam. Memories were still difficult to honestly confront. No one ever said thank you for your service. Once you were identified as a Vietnam veteran, a few might be bold enough (or insensitive enough) to ask if you considered going to Canada rather than get drafted. People often avoided mentioning this largely forgotten war because they felt that somehow our effort there had degraded our country's reputation. To make matters worse, there was the unstated but lingering criticism, sometimes from veterans of earlier wars, of why we didn't win the war. We won the two World Wars big time; what happened to you? Everyone knew that within twelve months of withdrawing our troops, the former country of South Vietnam was now part of a unified communist-run government, the very thing we tried to prevent. Saigon, the former capital of South Vietnam, had been renamed Ho Chi Minh City as an embarrassment to our country. Ho Chi Minh was the leader of the government and military fighting against a fledging, democratic South Vietnam and the United States. And even some Americans, like movie star Jane Fonda, applauded the resurgent communist nation of North Vietnam. [1]

Adding to the country's shocking disregard for its Vietnam veterans, President Jimmy Carter, on his first day in office in 1977, issued an unconditional pardon to an estimated forty to fifty thousand draft dodgers, men who had fled to Canada to avoid the military draft.[2] Even those men who broke the law by failing to register for the draft were given a pardon. Stop and think about the message sent to Vietnam veterans by those presidential actions. What a slap in the face to those who, while they may not have been in favor of the war, still gave two years of their life to serve their country honorably. What in the world was Carter (himself a World War II veteran) thinking? He certainly cared nothing about the feelings of the young veterans of this war. People I spoke with about President Carter's action (or lack of action) to help returning veterans agreed that he was less than forthright, sometimes promising help but rarely following through. To many of us his unconditional pardon was unconscionable.

The ironic part of this story about the draft dodgers was the public response by Vietnam veterans. When someone would ask them what they thought about young men fleeing to Canada to avoid the draft, most veterans, myself included, took a conciliatory tone. I often said, "It's OK. Most of these people were following their consciences against fighting in the war. That's their choice." My feelings about President Carter's actions, however, were quite different. I believed the president's unconditional pardon showed an unfeeling disregard and great disrespect for the sacrifices made by the soldiers who served. I believed these draft dodgers should be welcomed home only under certain conditions. They should be required to give two years of service to their country in some non-military capacity, such as VISTA or the Peace Corps. Even though I felt strongly that President Carter was wrong, I only would make that comment to another veteran.

We all came home questioning the necessity of the Vietnam War and also the futility of our efforts to fight and win the contest. By 1970 so many military restrictions were initiated that we felt we were fighting with one arm tied behind our collective back. One such regulation required we not fire on a suspected enemy unless we could positively identify he was an enemy soldier and that he was armed! You can imagine what the average American soldier thought about such limitations in battle. You can't fight a war like that.

We didn't love the devastations of war and we didn't love being away from home and our families for a year, but we answered the call when our country asked us to serve. We were a combination of raw, country boys and street-wise guys from all over the United States, a mixture of races, many not well educated. But most of all, we were from the lower economic stratum of society—*no money, no power, no connections.* We didn't ask to go to war, but we were the ones asked to make the sacrifice. In other wars a twenty-five-year old male was embarrassed not to be in the military. Questions for them were: "What's wrong with you? Why aren't you fighting for the country?" In the Vietnam era, the question was usually the reverse.

President Ronald Reagan said in his 1988 Veteran's Day speech, "Young Americans must never again be sent to fight and die unless we are prepared to let them win." And, I would add, we must be able to clearly pre-define what winning looks like. The president was correct in the sense that we were pawns in the hands of politicians who wouldn't know a deadly land mine from a coal mine. Why would we expect them to know anything about fighting or winning a war like this one; they couldn't possibly understand.

Combat veterans also made distinctions, probably unfairly, between themselves and those who spent their time in Vietnam in the rear areas, not seeing any "real action." There was a hierarchy, a kind of combat bravado, that was real for most guys. We were the fighters; they were the support people. We put our lives on the line daily; they hunkered down safely in secure rear bases. We slept on the ground often under fire; they slept in peaceful comfort ... and the list goes on. When I returned to Fort Carson for my final months on active duty, I did not salute any Army officer unless he had a Combat Infantry Badge (CIB). I figured they had not done anything to earn my respect. I did salute any Marine officer I crossed paths with because I had great respect for all the fighting Marines I met in Vietnam. These guys were tough and in the field were aggressively looking to engage the enemy. My wife constantly worried about this somewhat immature behavior on my part that might get me into trouble. "Just salute them," she would admonish me. My snarky retort to her was, "What are they going to do, send me back to Vietnam?" When I put my mind to it, I could be obnoxiously cocky with my combat-pedigree mentality. Fortunately, I never got confronted by any officer for not saluting. They often gave the Vietnam veterans some leeway (perhaps they were a little wary of these crazy combat veterans).

Don't Ask Me to Explain the War

We didn't want to talk about our experiences in Vietnam. Just keep your mouth shut. Don't engage in Vietnam conversations with these civilians—even friends—if they ever want to raise the issue. Why? Because they couldn't possibly even begin to understand what the soldier endured in Vietnam. They want to talk academically about the politics, the history of the conflict in Indo-China, the comparison of communism versus democracy, and so on. These academic topics are of little or no interest to the typical combat soldier. Did they ever see a friend die from a mortar attack? Did they ever have a friend die from an exploded grenade while you held him in your arms waiting for a Medevac helicopter to arrive? Did they ever see a friend get one of their legs blown off from an exploded mine? Did they ever see a friend get killed by a sniper's bullet? Of course not. And why would I, or any Vietnam vet, want to try to explain the heart-wrenching, unexplainable details to someone who may be innocently well-intentioned but is clueless. Life and death are serious and real every single day to a soldier in combat; political discussions are for those who are safely detached and only intellectually interested in the plight of those fighting the war. "Don't ask me to explain it to you," I thought to myself. I wasn't angry with the few people who dared to talk about Vietnam, I just didn't want to waste my time. Even if I could find the right words, they simply wouldn't understand.

It was particularly distressing for me to encounter people who wanted to marginalize the number of American casualties compared to all the Vietnamese soldiers and innocent citizens who were killed in the battles. I'm neither heartless nor unmoved by these numbers. One life lost in war—soldier or civilian—is a tragedy. But that fact does not alter my personal recollections and feelings about my friends and my comrades who were killed trying not to conquer a country but to defend it. Some people may believe the United States wanted their natural resources or that we were looking to gain some strategic military advantage in Southeast Asia. That is just not the case. Vietnam had no natural, cultural, or economic resources that were significant to our country. In 1954 we had formed the Southeast Asian Treaty Organization (SEATO) with nine other nations mainly to provide economic support and protection from military aggression from surrounding communist countries. In this war we were never a nation looking to expand the borders of our country or to bring Vietnam under the control of the United States. Our motives, however misapplied or misunderstood, remained to help this country fight communism and become a democratic country. And, although our actions likely were an overreach, we were not the bad guys here.

The Healing of a Nation Begins

President Reagan was highly regarded by most veterans. He saw the big picture. He understood the fact that we soldiers may not have loved fighting in this obscure Southeast Asian country, but we answered our country's call. How simple, yet profound and appreciated, was his attitude. On Veteran's Day, November 11, 1984, President Ronald Reagan formally accepted the Vietnam Veterans Memorial on behalf of the entire nation, not just the veterans. President Reagan had a rare gift to speak to and connect with the average citizen. He was generally admired as a former movie and television star, but he was fully embraced by the common man. He called the memorial a symbol of healing and a symbol of sacrifice for all Americans. Astoundingly, this memorial had been financed privately from over eight-million dollars of donations; not a penny of tax-payer money was used to plan, create, or build it. But it was President Reagan, speaking in his familiar warm, personal style, who claimed the memorial not only for the government but especially for the masses of Vietnam veterans whom he called heroes, soldiers worthy of our praise. Since the war's end, no other president or top-ranking national official had dared make such a statement. No one of his stature had ever used the word "hero" for this generation of fighters.

When President Reagan accepted the Vietnam Veterans Memorial for the country on that November morning, his speech along with the newly-constructed Memorial Wall started a process toward healing for our country:

> The war in Vietnam threatened to tear our society apart, and the political and philosophical disagreements that separated each side continue, to some extent. It's been said that these memorials reflect a hunger for healing. I don't know if perfect healing ever occurs, but I know that in one sense when a bone is broken and it is knit together well, it will in the end be stronger than if it had not been broken. I hope that before my days as Commander in Chief are ended the process will be completed.

> Let me say this to the Vietnam veterans gathered here today. When you returned home, you brought solace to the loved ones of those who fell, but little solace was given to you ... Some of your countrymen were unable to distinguish between their dislike for war and the stainless patriotism of those who suffered its scars. But there has been a rethinking there. Now we can say to you, and say as a nation, thank you for your courage. [3]

The president said the memorial reflects a "hunger for healing." Thus, in 1984, the healing for our nation and for our beleaguered veterans began in earnest.

In 1988 in his final Veterans Day speech as president, Reagan said:

> Unlike the other wars of this century ... there were deep divisions about the wisdom and rightness of the Vietnam War. Both sides spoke with honesty and fervor. And what more can we ask in our democracy. It was after all, however imperfectly pursued, the cause of freedom; and they [the soldiers] showed ***uncommon courage*** (emphasis mine) in its service...For a long time, they stood in a chill wind, as if on a winter's night watch. And in that night, their deeds spoke to us, but we knew them not. And their voices called out to us, but we heard them not...The night is over. We see these men and know them once again—and know how much we owe them, how much they have given to us, and how much we can never fully repay. And not just as individuals but as a nation, we say we love you.[4]

Is it any wonder why President Reagan's unusual appreciation for the sacrifices made by this generation of soldiers made him a hero for so many returning from Vietnam? Uncommon courage! In this time in our country, no one ever described us in this way. We appreciated that the President of the United States was not afraid to say it. And, he remains a genuine hero to this day for myself and so many other Vietnam veterans. Thank you, President Reagan.

Against All Odds - A Most Unlikely Hero

In 1970, a young enlisted man returned to his Maryland home from a twelve-month tour of duty in Vietnam. Specialist 4th Class Jan C. Scruggs, like so many others, served bravely and honorably with the 199th Infantry Brigade during his time in country. Jan was seemingly nobody special—he had no college degree, he had no commanding presence, his family was not wealthy or known in Washington politics (his father was a milkman), and he was not a highly-decorated soldier. Indeed, he was like so many soldiers, just a regular "Joe." But history would change that non-descript identification forever. Jan Scruggs became the visionary, the organizer, the fundraiser, and the laser-focused driver for what has become the most-visited memorial in our nation's capital, the Vietnam Memorial Wall. It is a most unlikely, seemingly implausible, story of the fierce determination of one man, capably aided by a strong coterie of political big shots, business executives, military brass, sharp legal minds and other gifted civic-minded volunteers whom he recruited.

Jan caught a vision, a dream, that drove him relentlessly and passionately over a period of thirty-five years. His vision came to him after watching the 1978 movie, "*The Deer Hunter,*" about many soldiers in Vietnam who were killed without any lasting recognition. He agonized over all his friends and comrades from his infantry unit who died while he served with them in country. Against all odds, Jan was able to bring his dream to fruition. His vision and his driving passion transformed into building a lasting, dignified memorial to honor the people who were killed in Vietnam in service to their country—all 58,000 of them. The vision was clear and, in some ways, even simple. The idea to "build it and they will come" happened long before the 1989 baseball movie *"A Field of Dreams"* was released. The purpose for the memorial was never to glamorize the war or to take one side or the other regarding the advisability of the conflict. It was simply to honor those who, when called by their country, served, fought, and died during this period in American history. Yet, from the very beginning, the wall would become a welcoming and comforting balm not just for the Vietnam veterans, but amazingly also as a symbol of reconciliation for people on both sides of the Vietnam War debate.

As would be expected in the morass of Washington life and politics, building such a monument would prove to be incredibly complicated. The obstacles Scruggs encountered from all potential stakeholders were staggering—from often intractable elected officials and life-long bureaucrats, from veterans' groups who wanted money spent to improve benefits to veterans not on memorials (even though no government money was being spent), from anti-war protesters who detested any recognition for what they viewed as an immoral war, from rich and powerful national leaders, and from military hawks and doves who had their own divisive objectives. Many thought he was wacky or just plain naïve, if not wild-eyed looney. None of that negativity got in his way. Scruggs persisted in ways that, in retrospect, seem incredibly difficult and even impossible. Against all odds, Spec 4 (now private citizen) Jan Scruggs succeeded beyond anyone's imagination ... except perhaps his.

By the force of his strong will and focus and with significant help from capable, well-connected people who bought into his vision, most notably including Senators Charles Mathias (R-MD) and Sen John Warner (R-VA), the Vietnam Memorial Wall was erected three and one-half years after Scruggs and a small but dedicated group of volunteers announced his plan. Mathias and Warner were from different political persuasions and had different views about the Vietnam War. Mathias was a hawk; Warner was a dove. Senator George McGovern (D-SD), the Democratic nominee for president in 1968, was an active opponent of the war. Yet at the urging of Scruggs, McGovern strongly supported building the Vietnam Memorial to honor those who died. These differences helped forge a diverse coalition of people with broadly differing views of the war to build an appropriate memorial recognizing those who were killed in service to their country.

By all accounts the time frame for this endeavor would prove to be unprecedented. Scruggs and his committee announced the plans on Memorial Day 1979. They set a three-year completion goal—an impossible task by bureaucratic Washington standards no matter who was leading the request. By comparison, the Lincoln Memorial was proposed in 1867 and not completed until 1922, a long time-frame even by Washington standards, but representative of the usual painfully slow pace of completion for this type of project in our nation's capital. Among other improbabilities ... the wall was constructed on the Constitution Mall between the Lincoln and Washington monuments, prime real estate and the precise location Scruggs and his committee had desired and lobbied for. Scruggs had turned down other suggested locations including the more remote Arlington Cemetery, thereby risking the entire project. He refused the site, saying, "We mustn't let them stick our memorial in such an out-of-the-way place. It must be where people will see it." [5] He knew what he wanted and where he wanted it; he stayed fiercely focused and determined to pursue the dream as he saw it.

The selection of the winning design for the wall is another mind-boggling, improbable story rife with divisiveness, racial overtones, and power struggles. Scruggs' committee, organized as the Vietnam Memorial Fund, had selected an august group of American art experts to judge the submissions for the memorial design. A gigantic airplane hangar at Andrews Air Base was needed in order to set up all of the over 1,400 submitted designs. The competition drew this large number of submissions from some nationally-known artists and from scores of unknown ones. They were displayed without attribution as to the designer to prevent any bias from the judges. During the process as the judges began whittling down the submissions, they kept commenting on one unusual design. After several days of deliberations, the judges unanimously settled on their choice. They selected the unusual work submitted by Maya Lin, a twenty-year old architectural student from Yale.

Once announced, the selection created a maelstrom of negative criticism from an unusually broad spectrum of constituencies. The winning design was made from rectangular panels of black granite shaped in a form similar to the letter "V' and would be cut almost unobtrusively into a gently bowed landscape. The names of all the people killed in Vietnam would be engraved into the panels. Because art can be interpreted so personally, any unusual piece of artwork— just because it is art—is likely to be heavily criticized, and this one was no exception. The *Washingtonian* magazine referred to "Vietnam, America's most unpopular war and the nation's most divisive monument."[6] Tom Carhart, a Vietnam veteran, West Point graduate, and influential member of the Memorial Foundation planning team described the design as a "black gash of shame."[7]

There were also, of course, many positive articles and reviews from newspapers like the *New York Times* that noted [the design's] "extreme dignity and restraint honors these veterans with more poignancy, surely, than more conventional monuments...."[8] Syndicated columnist James Kilpatrick wrote most presciently, "This will be the most moving war memorial ever erected."[9]

Negative feedback came from diverse segments of interested parties including powerful financial contributors, veterans' groups, and politicians. Eventually, two of the most vocal and formidable critics Scruggs had to overcome were the billionaire and future presidential candidate, H. Ross Perot, and Republican Senator and former Vietnam POW John McCain. They vigorously opposed the design. Jan Scruggs versus two of the most powerful and influential men in our country. Who do you think would win this battle? Well, as it turns out, Jan Scruggs should not have been underestimated. He proved tougher and more determined than any of his influential foes. These two men, Perot and McCain, represented money and power and they, along with others, favored a traditional design with statues of soldiers; they thought the winning design was a dark, depressing wall of shame. Ironically enough, Perot had actually financed the contest to choose the winning design with a contribution of one-hundred-sixty-thousand dollars. Once again, a determined Specialist 4 Jan Scruggs, who by this time had earned his law degree, persisted and outlasted and outmaneuvered his foes.

I had the pleasure of spending a brief time with Jan Scruggs. When I contacted him to say I was writing a book about Vietnam and would like to talk with him, he invited me to his home in Maryland. At this stage of his life, Jan seems somewhat oblivious to how unprecedented was the vision and subsequent journey of his to build this lasting memorial.

Oh, he will take credit for many things that were required to make the memorial happen and give appropriate credit to an outstanding and dedicated group of workers. But he seems almost casually unaffected by the magnitude of his efforts. This was a young man without real credentials, without national influence, without initial support from powerful politicians, and without financial means to complete his singular vision to recognize those killed in service to the country. Think about those non-credentials. For this seemingly average citizen and former soldier to successfully bring this formidable vision to fruition against all odds is, in the opinion of this writer, one of the more amazing American entrepreneurial success stories in our history. Over five million people per year visit this wall! It is a symbol of healing and reconciliation for our country. The powerful impact on those who view it is incalculable. The cost to the taxpayer was *zero* (as in nothing, since all funds were privately raised.)

Over eight million dollars was eventually raised for the construction of this site. Most of the contributions came in the form of small donations from people around the nation. Senators Warner and Mathias were helpful in raising some larger donations from private sources. Senator Warner, married to Elizabeth Taylor at the time, told Scruggs that to raise money the senator would invite local CEOs to his home for a fund-raising brunch. The brunch drew a large crowd of important business leaders. Scruggs told me that when Elizabeth Taylor came strolling down their long staircase in a beautiful robe these big-shot CEOs jaws dropped to the floor at the sight of the glamorous movie star. She was a show-stopper. Both Senator Warner and Elizabeth Taylor were two of the biggest supporters and largest contributors to funding the Vietnam Memorial Wall. In his own words, Jan told me when he grabs hold of an idea he is focused, determined, and relentless. Who could dispute those characteristics? Nothing stopped him. He never lost focus on the ultimate objective. It would seem that he was singularly destined to conceive and to create this wonderful, lasting memorial. This man is a hero to Vietnam veterans today. Thank you, Jan Scruggs.

Hate the War but not the Soldier

How was it that by the beginning of the 1990s our nation felt differently about the soldiers who fought in Vietnam? By then, the scars and divisions that had embroiled our country for so long had long begun to heal. Lessons were learned from this terribly divisive experience that would be applied in the future. Combat troops were called up in 1990 during the Gulf War, another war that was not universally accepted in our country. Anti-war protesters again went to the streets. This time, however, protesters made the critical distinction between a war they did not favor and the soldier who was called to duty. Hate the war but not the soldier! It seems the country had learned an important lesson. Undoubtedly, time also was an important factor in changing people's attitudes between 1970 and 1990. Memories, even bad ones, began to fade over that twenty-year period.

Beyond the natural passage of time were two figures who were preeminent in changing the attitudes about the Vietnam War and the soldiers who fought in that war. President Reagan is ranked by most historians as one of the top ten presidents in our history. [10] Early in his presidency, he had the courage to express his admiration, support, and appreciation to the Vietnam soldier before any other national figure dared to do so. And he was a master communicator. Jan Scruggs is an American hero. His legacy and the Vietnam Memorial Wall will be a part of American history forever.

These two forces—a United States president and an unknown combat veteran—opened the door for our nation to begin to heal. President Reagan through his attitude, words, and actions brought comfort and healing to a nation in need of both. Vietnam veteran Jan Scruggs drove a group of dedicated leaders with uncompromising energy to build a lasting memorial.

How unlikely a story. Today, the Vietnam Memorial Wall is honored as a hallowed sanctuary by many veterans and civilians and recognized as one of the best-designed monuments of the twentieth century. [11] So much of the American spirit of personal responsibility, optimism, and persistence is embodied by these two men and their accomplishments and accountability. All veterans and fair-minded people of this country owe them their sincere gratitude. I salute them both.

Picture with Dad and me one year before his death.

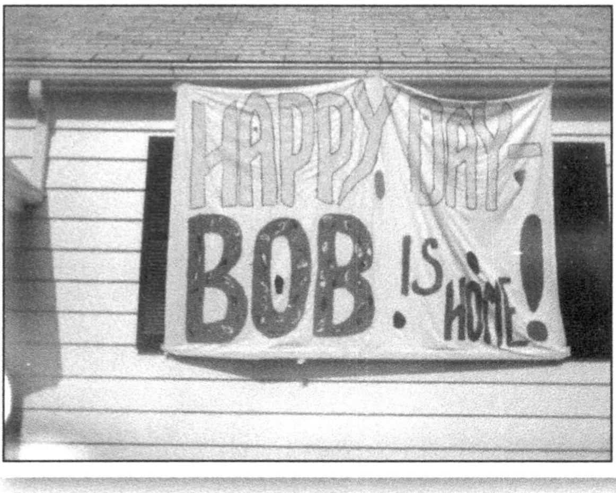

Connie put up a huge (10' x 8') banner on the front of her parents' house welcoming me home.

Connie is showing off our new Fisher state of the art stereo sound system which I ordered from overseas at a highly discounted price. We used this equipment for over twenty-five years.

Lynette, Connie's younger sister, and me standing outside Connie's parents' home in Rock Island, shortly after I returned from Vietnam.

Picture with my mom who lived in Nashville, Tennessee.

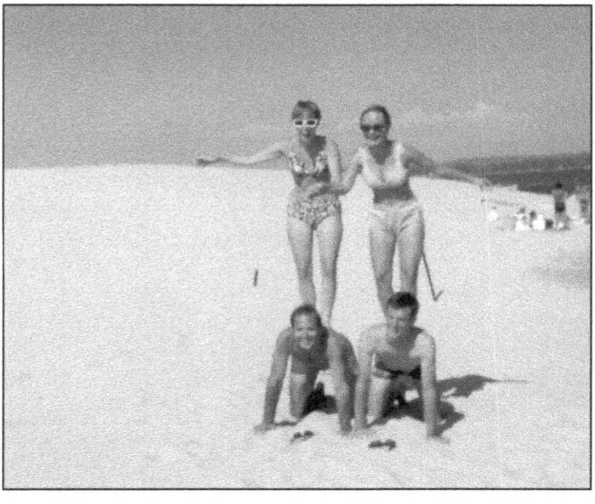

During my leave, Connie and I drove to Michigan to spend a long weekend with our college friends Bob and Cindy Deffenbaugh.

THE UNITED STATES OF AMERICA

TO ALL WHO SHALL SEE THESE PRESENTS, GREETING:

THIS IS TO CERTIFY THAT
THE PRESIDENT OF THE UNITED STATES OF AMERICA
AUTHORIZED BY EXECUTIVE ORDER, 24 AUGUST 1962
HAS AWARDED

THE BRONZE STAR MEDAL

TO

SERGEANT ROBERT M. GIVENS, UNITED STATES ARMY

FOR
MERITORIOUS ACHIEVEMENT
IN GROUND OPERATIONS AGAINST HOSTILE FORCES
IN THE REPUBLIC OF VIETNAM FROM 1 JANUARY 1970 TO 30 APRIL 1970

GIVEN UNDER MY HAND IN THE CITY OF WASHINGTON
THIS FOURTH DAY OF AUGUST 1970

A. E. MILLOY
Major General, USA
Commanding

SECRETARY OF THE ARMY

Copy of the Vietnam Service Award with the Bronze Star Medal for service in the Vietnam War.

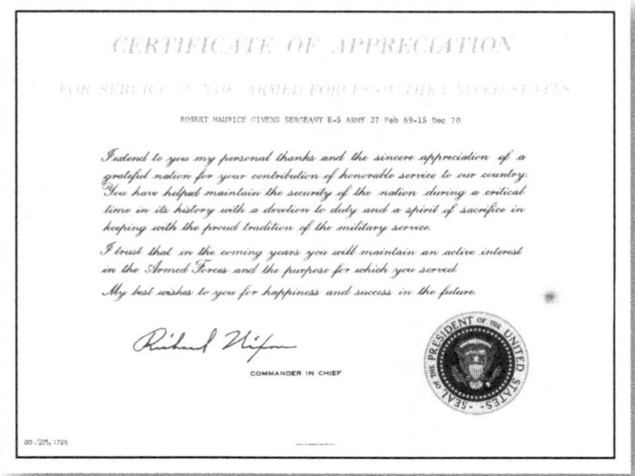

CERTIFICATE OF APPRECIATION

FOR SERVICE IN THE ARMED FORCES OF THE UNITED STATES

ROBERT MAURICE GIVENS SERGEANT E-5 ARMY 27 Feb 69-15 Dec 70

I extend to you my personal thanks and the sincere appreciation of a grateful nation for your contribution of honorable service to our country. You have helped maintain the security of the nation during a critical time in its history with a devotion to duty and a spirit of sacrifice in keeping with the proud tradition of the military service.

I trust that in the coming years you will maintain an active interest in the Armed Forces and the purpose for which you served.

My best wishes to you for happiness and success in the future.

COMMANDER IN CHIEF

Army Certificate of Appreciation issued after my discharge from the service.

This isn't the Jaguar XKE that I was dreaming about in Vietnam but I loved this sporty and fast 1970 Chevy Camaro. We named the car Jethro.

Visiting with Jan Scruggs at his home. Jan is the visionary and driver behind the Vietnam Memorial Wall in Washington D.C. The work Jan and his team of (mostly) volunteers carried out to get this memorial built is an amazing story.

A picture of the Vietnam Memorial Wall, located on the National Mall in Washington D.C., the most visited memorial in our nation's capital.

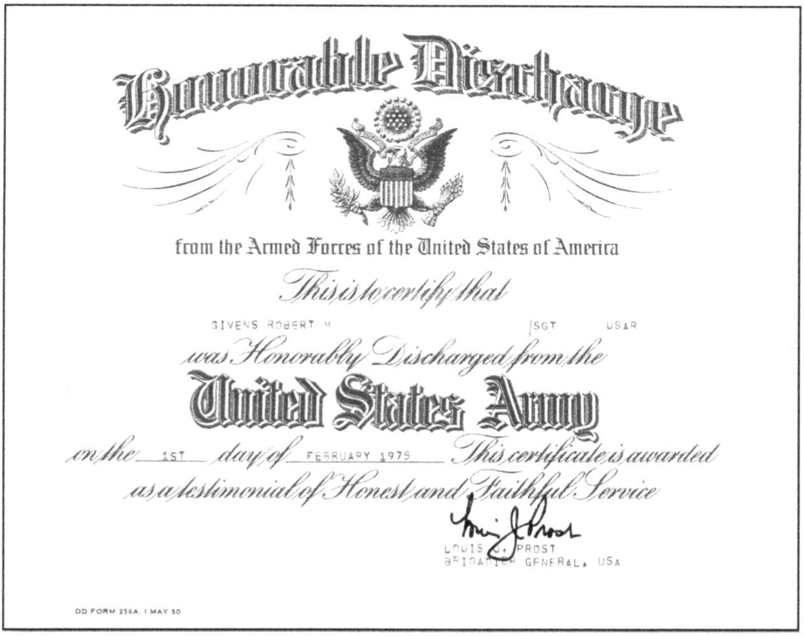
Honorable Discharge

from the Armed Forces of the United States of America

This is to certify that

GIVENS ROBERT M 1SGT USAR

was Honorably Discharged from the

United States Army

on the 1ST day of FEBRUARY 1975 This certificate is awarded

as a testimonial of Honest and Faithful Service

LOUIS J. PROST
BRIGADIER GENERAL, USA

DD FORM 256A, 1 MAY 50

A copy of my Honorable Discharge from the U.S. Army dated February 1, 1975.

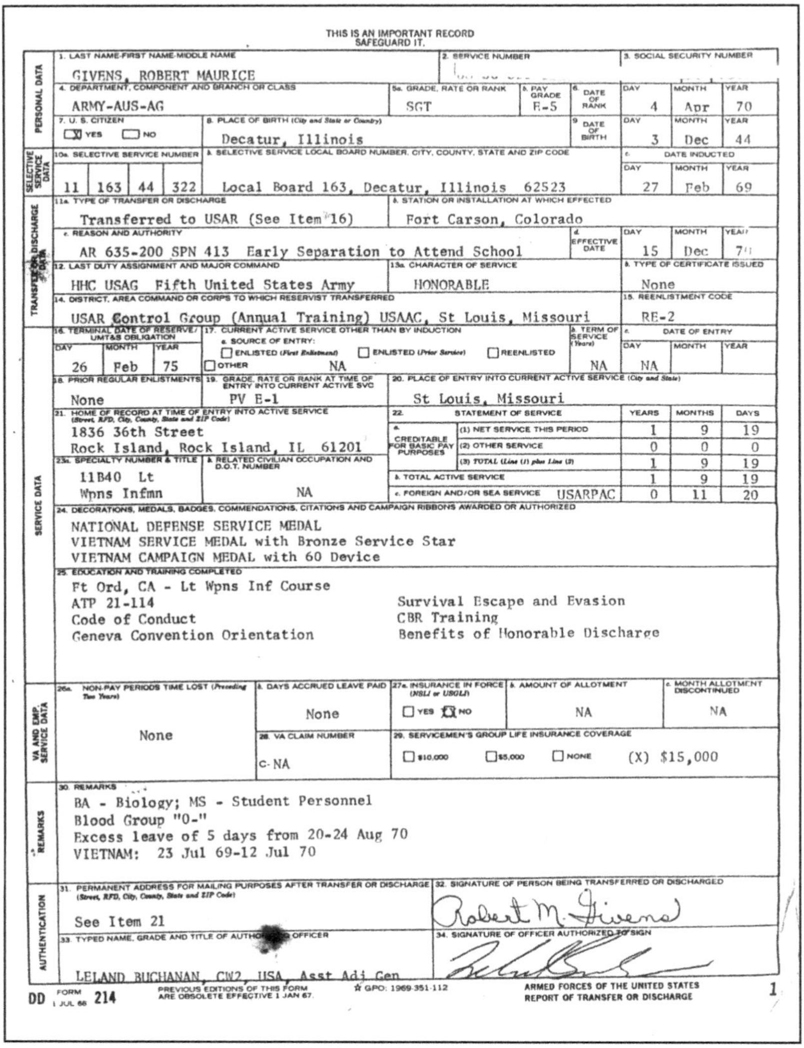

THIS IS AN IMPORTANT RECORD
SAFEGUARD IT.

PERSONAL DATA

1. LAST NAME-FIRST NAME-MIDDLE NAME: GIVENS, ROBERT MAURICE
2. SERVICE NUMBER:
3. SOCIAL SECURITY NUMBER:
4. DEPARTMENT, COMPONENT AND BRANCH OR CLASS: ARMY-AUS-AG
5a. GRADE, RATE OR RANK: SGT
b. PAY GRADE: E-5
6. DATE OF RANK: DAY 4 MONTH Apr YEAR 70
7. U. S. CITIZEN: [X] YES [ ] NO
8. PLACE OF BIRTH (City and State or Country): Decatur, Illinois
9. DATE OF BIRTH: DAY 3 MONTH Dec YEAR 44

SELECTIVE SERVICE DATA

10a. SELECTIVE SERVICE NUMBER: 11 163 44 322
b. SELECTIVE SERVICE LOCAL BOARD NUMBER, CITY, COUNTY, STATE AND ZIP CODE: Local Board 163, Decatur, Illinois 62523
c. DATE INDUCTED: DAY 27 MONTH Feb YEAR 69

TRANSFER OR DISCHARGE DATA

11a. TYPE OF TRANSFER OR DISCHARGE: Transferred to USAR (See Item 16)
b. STATION OR INSTALLATION AT WHICH EFFECTED: Fort Carson, Colorado
c. REASON AND AUTHORITY: AR 635-200 SPN 413 Early Separation to Attend School
d. EFFECTIVE DATE: DAY 15 MONTH Dec YEAR 70
12. LAST DUTY ASSIGNMENT AND MAJOR COMMAND: HHC USAG Fifth United States Army
13a. CHARACTER OF SERVICE: HONORABLE
b. TYPE OF CERTIFICATE ISSUED: None
14. DISTRICT, AREA COMMAND OR CORPS TO WHICH RESERVIST TRANSFERRED: USAR Control Group (Annual Training) USAAC, St Louis, Missouri
15. REENLISTMENT CODE: RE-2

SERVICE DATA

16. TERMINAL DATE OF RESERVE/UMT&S OBLIGATION: DAY 26 MONTH Feb YEAR 75
17. CURRENT ACTIVE SERVICE OTHER THAN BY INDUCTION
a. SOURCE OF ENTRY: [ ] ENLISTED (First Enlistment) [ ] ENLISTED (Prior Service) [ ] REENLISTED [ ] OTHER NA
b. TERM OF SERVICE (Years): NA
c. DATE OF ENTRY: DAY NA MONTH YEAR
18. PRIOR REGULAR ENLISTMENTS: None
19. GRADE, RATE OR RANK AT TIME OF ENTRY INTO CURRENT ACTIVE SVC: PV E-1
20. PLACE OF ENTRY INTO CURRENT ACTIVE SERVICE (City and State): St Louis, Missouri
21. HOME OF RECORD AT TIME OF ENTRY INTO ACTIVE SERVICE (Street, RFD, City, County, State and ZIP Code): 1836 36th Street, Rock Island, Rock Island, IL 61201

22. STATEMENT OF SERVICE		YEARS	MONTHS	DAYS
a. CREDITABLE FOR BASIC PAY PURPOSES	(1) NET SERVICE THIS PERIOD	1	9	19
	(2) OTHER SERVICE	0	0	0
	(3) TOTAL (Line (1) plus Line (2))	1	9	19
b. TOTAL ACTIVE SERVICE		1	9	19
c. FOREIGN AND/OR SEA SERVICE	USARPAC	0	11	20

23a. SPECIALTY NUMBER & TITLE: 11B40 Lt Wpns Infmn
b. RELATED CIVILIAN OCCUPATION AND D.O.T. NUMBER: NA
24. DECORATIONS, MEDALS, BADGES, COMMENDATIONS, CITATIONS AND CAMPAIGN RIBBONS AWARDED OR AUTHORIZED:
NATIONAL DEFENSE SERVICE MEDAL
VIETNAM SERVICE MEDAL with Bronze Service Star
VIETNAM CAMPAIGN MEDAL with 60 Device
25. EDUCATION AND TRAINING COMPLETED:
Ft Ord, CA - Lt Wpns Inf Course
ATP 21-114
Code of Conduct
Geneva Convention Orientation
Survival Escape and Evasion
CBR Training
Benefits of Honorable Discharge

VA AND EMP. SERVICE DATA

26a. NON-PAY PERIODS TIME LOST (Preceding Two Years): None
b. DAYS ACCRUED LEAVE PAID: None
27a. INSURANCE IN FORCE (NSLI or USGLI): [ ] YES [X] NO
b. AMOUNT OF ALLOTMENT: NA
c. MONTH ALLOTMENT DISCONTINUED: NA
28. VA CLAIM NUMBER: C- NA
29. SERVICEMEN'S GROUP LIFE INSURANCE COVERAGE: [ ] $10,000 [ ] $5,000 [ ] NONE (X) $15,000

REMARKS

30. REMARKS:
BA - Biology; MS - Student Personnel
Blood Group "O-"
Excess leave of 5 days from 20-24 Aug 70
VIETNAM: 23 Jul 69-12 Jul 70

AUTHENTICATION

31. PERMANENT ADDRESS FOR MAILING PURPOSES AFTER TRANSFER OR DISCHARGE (Street, RFD, City, County, State and ZIP Code): See Item 21
32. SIGNATURE OF PERSON BEING TRANSFERRED OR DISCHARGED: Robert M. Givens
33. TYPED NAME, GRADE AND TITLE OF AUTHORIZING OFFICER: LELAND BUCHANAN, CW2, USA, Asst Adj Gen
34. SIGNATURE OF OFFICER AUTHORIZED TO SIGN

DD FORM 1 JUL 68 214 PREVIOUS EDITIONS OF THIS FORM ARE OBSOLETE EFFECTIVE 1 JAN 67. ☆ GPO: 1969-351-112 ARMED FORCES OF THE UNITED STATES REPORT OF TRANSFER OR DISCHARGE 1

Copy of my DD 214 Certificate of Discharge from Military Duty.

Our daughters, Kierin and Stephanie, attending their grandparents 50th wedding anniversary in Rock Island, Illinois.

On vacation in Hawaii with Kierin, Stephanie and Dan Rice, and our five grandchildren: Caleb Rice, Luke Rice, Jack Caldwell, Sam Caldwell, and Allyson Caldwell.

I had a wonderful experience traveling to Uganda in 2008 with World Vision, the Christian organization that sponsors children around the globe.

My friend Bryden Carnahan and I attending graduation ceremonies at Millikin University in Decatur as part of the University's Board of Trustees.

Doug Shaw, my long-time business partner and co-founder of Monotype Imaging, in New York City the day our company went public on the NASDAQ exchange.

A family photo with Connie's parents, Glen and Dorothy Richeson, along with their three children, Connie, Dale Richeson and Lynette Richeson. In back is Lynette's husband, Rudy Kopecky, Lynette and her daughter Alissa Egert. In front are Dale, Kierin Givens, Stephanie and Dan Rice.

— EIGHT —

Life After Vietnam

Survivors

Soldiers' attitudes about the war in Vietnam were intensely personal; in most cases the experiences were life changing. The horrors of any war are not easily forgotten. After spending twelve months in the fields of Vietnam, no one came home unaffected. Physical and emotional scars were common and often deep. Survivors learned how best to deal with their own issues, whether that healing came from caring family members, professional support, or simply time. And, of course, not everyone recovered at the same rate. Some never recovered. Several veterans I corresponded with say even fifty years later they think about their wartime experiences every day; others say it took some time—years—to wipe out the difficult memories; and some like myself moved on, trying their best just to forget about it. Indeed, the war experience was intensely personal.

Every combat veteran learned during his tour of duty in Vietnam, often to his surprise, that he could adapt and survive while dealing with more hardships than he ever could have imagined. If on the flight to Vietnam, someone had told me what I would have to endure over the next six months, I probably would have said (only half-jokingly), "Just shoot me and get it over with." Actually, I surprised myself. I found I could drive myself much harder physically than I realized. I discovered I could adapt through instinct and determination to living in rugged, third-world-country conditions under constant stress that challenged and threatened me every day.

When we came home from the war, most of us also learned to survive the psychological impact of insults and reproach from the anti-war sentiments that divided the country. Over time attitudes were softened, as people learned to hate the war but not the soldier, and then transformed, as many are now able to say to me and other veterans, "Thanks for your service."

Starting My Career

Once my Army service ended at Ft. Carson, Colorado, I decided not to go back into higher education. The difficulties of trying to lead and inspire often disinterested students didn't offer the rewards I was looking for either vocationally or financially. Even at age twenty-six I thought a job in the university setting would be acceptable only if someone wanted to hire me as their president. Not likely! One thing I knew for certain: It was important for me to have control over my job and my life. I was tired of taking orders from the Army, from my school, or from anyone. I wanted to make my own decisions and be in charge of my own life—not an unreasonable attitude coming after twenty-four months under strict Army control. Many years later I would learn how unrealistic that attitude would prove to be in any business enterprise where, even when you run the company, you answer to bosses—either the bank, board members, stockholders, or all the above. But at age twenty-six, I was ready to conquer the world on my own terms. So, I enrolled in the MBA program at The University of Denver, mainly to utilize their job placement office to begin a business career where I could be, or at least become, the boss.

By the time I was eleven, my parents had divorced and I was living with my mother. In the formative years up to the time of my parents' separation, my dad impressed on me that you can do anything you set your mind to do. Key to his world view that he inculcated in me was, "Nobody will give you anything. You have to aggressively pursue your goals by working hard, never quitting, and not letting anyone stop you. You are in control of your own destiny." And he said, "Have fun while you're doing it." He adamantly instilled these attitudes in me until they were natural. I pretty much lived my life with that philosophy until ... it no longer worked for me.

Business classes at The University of Denver were both interesting and relatively easy for me. I'd already earned one master's degree and taken several business courses at Indiana University. I understood the five P's of marketing, MacGregor's Theory X and Theory Y of management, Maslow's hierarchy of needs, plus I had experiences managing people and activities at UConn. So I figured I was ahead of most other students. Through my work experiences I had learned and applied the principles of successful salesmanship, including understanding the importance of listening carefully to the customer. So now it was time to find the right business opportunity to begin my career (and eventually run the company!).

During the interview process, two companies interested me and both offered jobs in Denver. One was 3M, the international company best known for their Scotch Tape™ products; the other was a smaller regional company that sold synthetic turf surfaces for athletic fields. Everything about 3M interested me including the offer to be their sales representative responsible for sales in the states of Colorado and Wyoming. Besides a nice salary, commission, and a generous expense account, I was given a new Mercury Marquis for my company car that I could use for both business and personal driving. I more than doubled my compensation from the University of Connecticut job. And, in many ways, I was running my own little business. My boss lived in Minneapolis and only visited me three or four times a year. I worked out of our apartment and set my own schedule. Every month sales from my territory were calculated and published, so results were measurable and feedback was frequent. I flourished with this company and in this environment.

Six months after beginning my new job with 3M, we were ready to start a family. Our daughter, Kierin Lyn Givens, was born in November 1971. I made up Kierin's name from an Irish male name (Ciarán) and Lyn was after Connie's sister, Lynette. Connie had been working as a substitute teacher until a few months prior to Kierin's birth. For the next six years until we hit bottom financially, Connie worked diligently as a stay-at-home mom.

Over the next three years, I progressed rapidly in my job and became one of the leading sales representatives for 3M's Industrial Graphics Division. I loved the positive recognition and achievement rewards given me by 3M. In 1974, I was promoted by 3M to a marketing job in St. Paul, Minnesota, the home office. Connie was pregnant with our second child when we bought our first home in Eagan, Minnesota—a newly constructed three-bedroom, split-level home costing $34,500. The Veteran's Association (VA) home loan program was a great help to us, enabling the purchase of our house with no down payment. Our daughter Stephanie was born in September 1974, and our family was now four people and one dog (a Sheltie mix we named Denver).

This company was an outstanding one to jumpstart my business career. They taught me about the printing industry and provided excellent instruction to learn professional sales skills. I learned the business of the printing and, publishing world from them, and this industry would be at the center of my entire forty-five-year career. Alas! I ended up leaving 3M after spending one year at the home office in the marketing job. I wasn't ready yet for this kind of home office environment where my work was constantly monitored, scrutinized, and criticized on an almost daily basis. There was just too much close supervision to suit me at this point in my career. I cherished my freedom and independence more than this job offered—plus the winter was brutal. We still had snow covering our yard the first week of May. So I quit and took a job with one of my former distributors in Denver, a place we had lived for over four years and where we had acquired many friends and professional contacts.

Stressing our Marriage

The job in Denver lasted only about three months. Almost immediately I realized I had made a career mistake moving from a growing international company to a small, family-owned distributor of graphic arts products. I began interviewing again and accepted a new position with Compugraphic Corporation, an international manufacturer of typesetting equipment serving the printing industry. Compugraphic was much smaller than 3M but provided a nice career path for me with a good financial package.

There was a problem with this job; our family would have to move to the San Francisco area. Three different jobs in three states in one year is more than most marriages can withstand, and ours was rocked by these unsettling moves, my job instability, and a me-first attitude. My wife was being forced against her better judgment to sever all personal and professional relationships she had made over the past four years and move to the West Coast, where she did not know a soul. Connie, with two preschool children and our dog in tow, was rightfully upset and frustrated with me and my job-hopping quest for career fulfillment. A combination of factors was required to shake me out of the self-absorbed path I was following. My job, my desire to be the number-one sales person, my independence, and my career aspirations had all become more important to me than what should have mattered the most—my wife and family.

It took, literally, *acts of God* to shake me from this insidious, selfish lifestyle—not just one act of God, but a series of unlikely events. Driving my operating philosophy and actions were two well-developed attitudes: (1) my dad's admonition that I didn't need help from anyone, I was in total control of my life and would succeed or fail based solely on my own efforts, and (2) I believed religion was an unnecessary crutch weak-minded people (mostly losers) needed because they were unable to succeed on their own. In Vietnam my eyes had been surprisingly opened to the possibility of a God who actually intervened in our lives. In the four years following Vietnam, I did virtually nothing to proactively follow up on this personal insight, one that did not comfortably fit within my operating philosophy. As I continued in my successful business career, I still had an open mind about God but I was no longer seeking. My life changed in California … God began seeking me.

Three Moves/Three States/ Three Jobs/One year

First of all, God had to get our family to the right place and that proved to be Northern California. It was in this place and environment that I began moving from an intellectually committed agnostic—who thought he was so smart and self-sufficient he didn't need religion—to a dedicated Christian believer—who finally realized he needed a savior. The story has a number of unlikely twists and turns—all memorable to me and also life changing.

It was devastating. At the end of 1975 after three moves in one year, our lives and our marriage were on shaky grounds. It is painful for me remembering the magnitude of the sacrifices I asked my family to make to satisfy my misguided career aspirations. In May, 1975, we moved from Eagan, Minnesota, to Denver. We left our comfortable first home for a cramped two-bedroom apartment in Denver. Three months later, August 1975, I informed Connie (that is the correct subject and predicate—Connie was never consulted) we were moving twelve-hundred miles to San Francisco. There was no "we" in that decision. I was chasing my selfish and elusive career dreams. Without any honest and deliberate discussions, I was directing her to follow me in this most unsettling move. We knew absolutely no one in California; our apartment was even smaller than in Denver since everything was more expensive; Connie was trying as best she could to care for two pre-school children (and a dog) in a strange, new place; and I was away all day and some evenings consumed by my new job. She was rightfully sad, frustrated, and upset. I realized our eight-year marriage was in some trouble.

Mrs. Richards

The California lifestyle was strange for two born and bred Midwesterners. We thought we were somewhat liberal in our thinking—not in California. The culture was aptly illustrated by a fence around every yard, a materialistic outlook that valued "things" over people, and liberal attitudes about everything from drugs to money to sex. We were slightly overwhelmed by the differences between "hip" California values and the more traditional values of the Midwest. So, we made a decision to try to find a church where, maybe, we would meet people who loved and cared for their children in a way familiar to us. We settled on a large Presbyterian church in Fremont, where we lived. I was satisfied this church would be doctrinally safe and middle-of-the-road, with no raised hands in worship or people shouting unintelligible prayers. Of course, my attitude was somewhat cynical; still, God could use it to help us find a church.

And then we found Mrs. Richards! Kierin, our four-year-old daughter was shy and very particular about people she liked. We were not at all sure she would go to her Sunday School class with a strange teacher she had never met. We prepared ourselves for the worst. We were informed Kierin would be in Mrs. Richards' class. When we walked into the classroom, Kierin was behind her mother, hanging on tightly to her leg. Connie introduced her to the teacher. Mrs. Richards, standing about ten feet away, got down on one knee, held out her arms in an open, inviting way, and said in a soft gentle voice, "Kierin, I am so glad you are here today. Jesus loves you." Slowly, Kierin came out from behind her mother and to my astonishment walked toward the open arms of Mrs. Richards. Kierin reached for Mrs. Richards hand and the two of them turned their backs to us and walked away. I was not too sure about this "Jesus loves you" stuff, but it was clear to me that Mrs. Richards was a nice woman who loved children. We returned to the church the following Sunday. As we entered the classroom, Mrs. Richards again got down on one knee and, remembering Kierin's name, said, "Kierin, I am so glad to see you today, Jesus loves you." This time Kierin went running toward Mrs. Richards right into her open arms. The two of them turned and walked hand-in-hand to another area of the room. Wow! I was impressed.

After this experience, we began regularly attending church, first this one in Fremont and then later a Methodist church when we moved to our new home in Livermore, California. Mrs. Richards with her warm, loving attitude helped us see that attending church regularly was a good decision for us. Thereafter, wherever we lived, we made attending church a priority for our family.

Our church experience helped introduce us to a popular international Christian organization called Marriage Encounter that works with people in good marriages to make their marriages even better. Couples spend a long weekend away on a marriage retreat that emphasizes developing good communications skills between husband and wife. Although I was at first skeptical that this kind of program would be helpful to us, I was pleasantly surprised and impressed with the weekend and follow-up meetings. We learned to write a "love letter" to each other on various pre-selected topics and read those letters at the end of the day. Over the next four years we wrote almost daily love letters to each other and met weekly with a small group of like-minded couples. Marriage Encounter became an important part of our lives and provided us a tool to help better communicate our feelings to each other without being judgmental. We grew individually and our marriage was strengthened as a result of the years we spent with this organization. We would need that stronger relationship to help us through the next debilitating events for our family.

Business Failure

Up to this point in my life and career, I had rarely experienced failure. If I encountered a difficult problem, I would learn what I needed to learn, diligently apply myself to the task, and use extraordinary effort to overcome the issue. This pattern of self-reliance and maximum effort worked well for me my entire life. Based on my experiences in school and my career, when I fiercely applied myself in these ways, I succeeded. Throughout all my work experiences, I always had been a top performer. My first sales job was selling clothes during college at Bachrach's, a fine men's clothing store, where I consistently was one of the top sales people; my contributions and plans at the University of Connecticut were adopted and widely praised by the senior college administrators who wanted me to return to the job after military service; 3M recognized me as one of their top sales performers and promoted me in less than three years to the home office; during my first year at Compugraphic I was one of the leading salesmen in the Western Region. I was good at these jobs and expected success. I knew what was needed to perform at the highest levels to receive the recognition and financial rewards accompanying achievement.

So, imagine my consternation during my second year with Compugraphic when I began to fail in my work and I couldn't turn things around. My sales were under quota for four months in a row, an experience that was totally foreign to me. After a couple months of dismal results, I began to apply my laser-focus, bear-down mentality and maximum work ethic to my job. I did everything I had done in the past—working extra hours, making more sales calls, preparing better proposals, and even canceling any vacation. Nothing worked as my results continued to be under quota. To make matters worse, more than one-third of my compensation was based on being over quota. So, my poor performance at work began causing us severe financial problems at home. To make our mortgage payment one month, we had to cash in an insurance policy Connie's dad had purchased for her. We were on the verge of losing the house so Connie, still with two very young children, obtained a California state license and opened her own daycare business in our home. Every morning around 7:00 a.m. as I headed off to work, mothers would be dropping off their children to be cared for in our home. Every part of our home, yard, even garage was used as places for learning and play for the kids. There is nothing glamorous or easy for one person (even an experienced and effective elementary school teacher) to take care of six children for ten hours a day. But as long as I continued in my downward sales slump, we needed the extra income to pay the bills.

Faith Alive Seminar

During this difficult time, our church in Livermore sponsored a *Faith Alive* weekend seminar put on by an Episcopal church from Reno, Nevada. Connie wanted to attend because child care was provided and it would allow her some respite from her constant focus on children—and she could have some adult conversations. This weekend seemed acceptable to me because the speaker was a vice-president of marketing for IBM, so I might be interested to hear what he had to say. Also, the event was sponsored by the Episcopal Church, which made it acceptable to my still wary mind about religious radicals in California.

What follows is a direct excerpt from my book *Heir to the Kingdom p. 169-173*. I cannot relate this most important and transformational story any better than I did in that book.

> With open minds, we attended [the seminar]. Pat, the IBM executive and main speaker, did not disappoint.

He was smart and articulate, without trying to pour any religious doctrine down my throat. I listened attentively as he told stories of how he tackled serious issues during his business career and leaned heavily upon God to help him. That concept was foreign to me. At one point he told us about an aggressively difficult and unfair boss. I expected him to tell us how he successfully changed this man's terrible attitude or, better yet, maybe he even punched him out—how mature on my part! Instead, he spoke in detail about how God worked on him (Pat) to change his opinion and perspective of this ordeal and this unfair boss. I was dumbfounded by this strong, intelligent person resolving a tough situation in a manner so thoroughly unknown to me. And yet I remained intrigued.

Later this man shared his spiritual journey and how he had gone from a doubter to seeker to believer. In the course of this personal story, he described clearly and concisely the gospel message—the good news of the Bible. I was fascinated by the clarity of this message that I had heard during my childhood in bits and pieces. Jesus, the Messiah, had come to earth specifically and willingly to die for my sins (the righteous for the unrighteous.) His death paid the price for my unrighteousness. My only responsibility is to believe that He is who He says He is, and I will have everlasting life. The whole message was so clear and compelling that I wondered why I had never before fully grasped this concept.

At the end of his last talk, the speaker said we could pray for forgiveness of our sins and ask Jesus to come into our lives. We didn't need to come forward to the altar in the church, we could remain in our seats. I was not yet ready to make that kind of confession or commitment.

Several weeks later I found out that during this weekend Connie had indeed prayed that prayer.

Work "Probation"

During the course of that year, 1976-1977, my sales results and my attitude continued to spiral downward as I was moving into unchartered water. I was convinced that my territory (Oakland/Alameda County) was not economically vibrant enough to sustain a salesperson. But, of course, those kinds of excuses were rejected by my boss as merely whining and rationalization by a failing sales person (and even by me given my "no excuses" mentality.) I decided to work longer hours and continue to apply my hard-work, bear-down philosophy. That summer Connie and the girls flew back to Illinois for two weeks to see Connie's parents. I stayed in California figuring I could not afford to take any vacation time due to my poor sales numbers.

Our regional manager, Pete Kersten, flew in from Los Angeles and arranged a dinner meeting with me. I expected some kind of "you-can-do-it" pep talk. Instead Pete told me that I was being put on probation that could lead to termination if my results didn't improve. He warned that I needed to at least achieve my sales quota over the next three months and my performance would be closely monitored. I was almost in total shock when I returned home with my battered ego. "I don't even know how to spell probation," I angrily relayed to Connie. I was furious at my boss and this company. I was more determined than ever to regain my status as a top salesperson for Compugraphic and then personally tell Pete Kersten that I quit this rotten job.

Spiritual Transformation

Besides working extra hours to try to improve my job performance, I also was working to keep a positive attitude in the midst of these career and family difficulties. One evening I called Pat, the IBM executive who spoke at the *Faith Alive* weekend. When he answered, I told him who was calling and said, "I'm sure you don't remember me." "Oh no," he replied, "I remember you from our seminar in Livermore." I asked him if he ever traveled to the Bay Area and, if so, could we meet? His response was surprisingly quick, "Are you close to the monastery in Oakland," he asked. When I told him I drive by it every day on my way to work, he asked, "Can you meet me there the day after tomorrow?" We set up a time to meet on that day, Thursday morning.

I had many questions to ask Pat about how he perceived God truly working in his life. He thoughtfully answered each question and then asked where I was in my spiritual journey? I was open and seeking answers but still resistant to giving up any control in my life. I shared personal thoughts and concerns with him that morning that I had never really talked about before with anyone.

Pat listened carefully and stopped me at one point to say, "You need to forgive your mother. Will you pray with me right now to forgive her?" "What do I need to forgive her for?", I asked. Pat's response was profound and his exact words are engraved in my memory. "Forgive her for anything she did to offend you," he stated definitively. "I can do that," I said. And I prayed with him.

Pat then told me something that almost freaked me out. He said that the Lord had spoken to him on that Monday (the day before I called him) and told him he needed to be at this specific monastery in Oakland on Thursday, 200 miles from his home. He had never before been there and had no idea why, but he was certain that God was leading him to go there. Then the next day, I phoned him. Wow! I'd never heard anything like that before. As we were ending our time together, Pat asked me if I would like to pray for forgiveness and ask Jesus to come into my life. Although our time together had been personally and spiritually powerful and uplifting, I said, "No, I'm not ready to do that." We parted with a warm hug.

I was now at a crucial personal juncture—the intersection of a prolonged and unique business failure and some sort of spiritual awakening. Only in retrospect, with the benefit of time and perspective, could I even know enough to make such a statement. While I was in the midst of this personal transformation, the experience was mainly painful and confusing.

I grappled with this conundrum over the next few weeks. One day while working my temporarily-assigned sales territory in San Francisco, someone handed me a small tract entitled "Steps to Peace with God." I had been offered these religious tracts many times before and always rejected them. This day I took one and placed it in the glove compartment of my car. Nothing had changed with our family finances—we were barely able to keep up with our bills. Professionally and personally I was at a low point—despondent over my failure not only with my business life but also with my family. The words and feeling of being a failure were no longer foreign to me.

A few weeks later, before beginning my one-hour drive to work in San Francisco, I pulled out the tract from my glove compartment and read through the "Steps to Peace with God." As I drove into the city, I was overcome with my terrible plight and circumstances; tears streamed down my face uncontrollably. I began praying and pleading with God that I needed help. I was not even aware of the other cars or my surroundings until I was stopped in traffic on the Oakland Bay Bridge. With eyes full of tears and a genuinely repentant heart, I prayed desperately to God. "God," I cried out audibly, "if you are real, would you come into my life and take control? I am messing up my family and failing in my work. I need you to take control of this out-of-control life." As I prayed this prayer, I envisioned me lifting my hands off of the steering wheel and God placing His hands there and taking control. With my vision acting as a reassurance that God heard my prayer, I ended by saying, "Thank you, God."

Words don't really matter to God; heart attitude does. My words may well have been theologically immature and even included the conditional phrase, "if you are real." God could not care less. He looked straight at my heart, my mind, my contrition, and my attitude at that moment and graciously accepted me just as I am—complete with many faults, failures, and doubts. There were no transformational lightning bolts during this time. But there was for me a realization that something significantly important had occurred. I was personally and profoundly impacted by this conversation with God. I realized I was giving up full control of my life and circumstances with my prayer to this God I was just beginning to know. That surrender required maximum effort on my part because it required me to let go a part of my life-long operating philosophy—nobody is going to give you anything, you must earn it and you are in control of your own destiny. Predictably, I was physically and mentally exhausted after this encounter and didn't yet know exactly what had happened or how my life might be changed.

It was weeks before I told Connie about this intensely personal experience with God. She was encouraging and confided with me her own story about accepting the invitation to receive Christ that was offered at the *Faith Alive* weekend. Our financial problems were still prevalent in our life but we both had experienced some form of spiritual awakening that we knew was going to be significant to us individually and as a family. We were open to the possibilities but clueless as to what they might be.

Dealing with Mom

By early 1978, Mom had been living in Nashville for almost ten years, and she had recently retired from her job as a bookkeeper at Hardaway Construction Company. My brother, Charles, no longer lived in Nashville as he had moved his family to Florida in the mid-seventies. Once Mom retired from work, she began drinking much earlier in the day. Sometimes she would fall in her apartment but was able get to a phone and call the police who would respond. I flew into Nashville to check on her after a business meeting in Massachusetts. The landlord confronted me and said that your mother needed to move immediately from the apartment. With her deteriorating health condition, he would no longer allow her to live by herself in this apartment. The conversation with the landlord occurred early on a Saturday morning in February. I was beside myself, distraught at the prospect of trying to deal with this impossible situation. I needed to get back to work in California and my mother was now homeless. What was I to do?

Before calling Connie, I sat alone and considered the alternatives available. I felt extremely anxious about what to do with my Mom. I wanted to do everything necessary to keep her in Nashville and have someone else deal with the issue. The problem, of course, was that there was no one else to help. My brother was out of the picture living in Florida and going through a divorce. Mom was now falling frequently and needed care; there was no realistic way she could remain in that apartment. Because of her disability and the timeframe mandated by the landlord, I concluded that no living arrangement for Mom in Nashville was going to work. The last thing in the world I wanted to do was the only alternative that seemed remotely feasible. I was going to have to bring Mom to California to live with us. That scenario was painful even to consider. I so disliked the thought of being responsible (again!) for my mother. She could be relentlessly high-maintenance. And, to make matters worse, my mother may have been the only person in the world who didn't like Connie. On a few occasions, while under the influence of alcohol, Mom had lashed out verbally at Connie. Her only excuse (which really was no excuse at all) was that Connie stole her baby. Her attitude and tone were mean-spirited and without any provocation. Connie was terribly and understandably hurt by the unreasonable attacks.

I called Connie to let her know the problems I was facing. I explained the situation in detail to her and then droned on with self-pity about all the alternatives I had considered since getting notice from the landlord that morning. Connie let me talk it through. Then she calmly stated that, of course, I needed to bring my mother to California. That was the right decision. We would work it out. She kept assuring me that everything would be alright. She would make our three-bedroom home ready for my mother to live there. "Don't worry," Connie kept repeating, "we'll be able to make this work. Everything will be fine." I was so full of despair and doubt but Connie's words of assurance gradually lightened my burden. I did not know how this arrangement could possibly work, but my wife was efficiently responding and even taking charge to make sure we would all be able to handle the situation. Thankfully, I had married well.

Connie moved the girls together into one bedroom and fixed up the third bedroom for Mom. Connie graciously welcomed my mother into our home; she worked diligently and, more than anyone, made the arrangement work. After three months we found Mom a nice apartment three blocks away from us. I watched in amazement as Connie continued to serve my mother day after day. She managed Mom and her apartment with care and great skill. Without complaining, she shopped and cooked for her, arranged for people to come visit who took care of little chores, and provided some companionship for my mother. "How could this be?" I thought. My wife is reaching out to my mother in a loving and caring way even though my mother didn't show her any genuine affection. And then it struck me; Connie is displaying the very essence of Christian love—loving and caring for someone who is not showing appreciation in return. Connie's acts of sacrificial love made a tremendous impression on me, and, to this day, I am so appreciative of the lessons she taught me with her unrequited graciousness and compassion.

Several months after Mom moved into the apartment, Connie confronted her about the problems her drinking was causing in our household. Sometimes in the middle of the night, my mother would fall getting up to go to the bathroom. She would reach the phone and call our house. I would have to drive to her apartment and help her back to bed. Connie was rightfully upset with my mother and the problems she was causing. Connie told her that she would ensure that no more alcohol would be allowed into her apartment. All of the people who brought her alcohol would be notified. This "tough love" approach eventually forced my mother to check herself into a six-week alcohol rehabilitation program at a local hospital. In July 1979, I drove her to the program, and, after she was released six weeks later, she never drank another drop of alcohol. Unfortunately, her health had deteriorated to the point that she died within sixty days of leaving the hospital.

Living My New Faith

God used each of these major, somewhat improbable, events to teach me invaluable life lessons and to draw me closer to Him. I needed the push. I was too entrenched in my self-absorbed, self-reliant, "smartest-guy-in the room" mentality. I would not have changed my life focus without His help. My dependence on myself would never have allowed me to recognize how much I needed a savior. After God captured my attention, everything was different—my life, my perspective on events, my relationship with others, my marriage, my love for family, and my work attitude. I was a changed person. I had grown to understand that dependency on a savior was surprisingly liberating for someone who thought it would be the exact opposite. I did not have to be perfect (I certainly was not) or even religious (whatever that meant.) I could just be myself. I was following a God who clearly demonstrated He loved me by sacrificing His son Jesus for my sins. I was able to see how God had remarkably intervened in my life. I desired to live according to His will, and when I failed in those efforts (and I did fail a lot) He would forgive me. And so, I grew in my faith and began to live my life differently.

God graciously provided me some examples to follow in my new-found faith. I am particularly thankful that I was able to build relationships with many (mostly older) men who lived Godly lives. All these men, influential to my life, were teachers of the Bible, through actual Bible studies and/or through their exemplary lives. I watched them and learned how they dealt with difficult times and how they responded to God's call in their lives. Their lives were inspirational to me. We all need heroes and God provided some for me.

Church became important in our lives so, no matter where we lived or moved, finding a church that believed in and taught the Bible was always a priority for our family. Our church in Livermore, California, provided us a foundation for beginning a lifelong journey of sharing lives with other people trying to live out their Christian faith. We loved the lessons learned from our experiences including understanding the power of the gospel message itself and living what the Bible calls the fruits of the spirit—love, joy, peace, patience, kindness, goodness, faithfulness, gentleness, and self-control. The fact that so many people, including avid church-goers, do not exhibit these traits is only partially a knock against the church, It is a testimony more to the fallibility of all of us and how much we need guidance and forgiveness from our savior.

I learned not to compartmentalize my faith—living out my faith was a full-time job and meaningful for every part of my life. It wasn't a church thing or a Sunday thing. Doing the best I could to live out my faith every day in every aspect of my life—work, family, and recreation—was "my thing."

Finishing Strong

Throughout my life and business career, I never outgrew my desire to be in control. I learned there were many times where it either was not necessary or desirable for me to be in charge. Other people may be better equipped and more experienced than I. Delegating responsibility became easier for me, especially going through the normal trials during my experiences at work and with raising a family.

Above everything, I realized and acknowledged that God was in control. It took years for me to fully comprehend that His plan for my life and His ultimate leadership was much better than anything I could have envisioned. Some days I may try to contest His control, but those are the times I remind myself—God has this situation/problem covered. He can handle it much better than I. And, He has my best interests in mind. I, of course, need to do my part and use all the skills and experiences that I have acquired ... but always following His leadership. I never question how much God loves me—that love has been well-proven. My constant goal is to live up to the lofty, providential expectations He has for me.

EPILOGUE

In September 2019, I was searching the Vietnam Memorial Wall website looking for Larry Betts' inscription. The 50th anniversary of Larry's death was coming up soon. People often leave short notes to the fallen soldiers on these sites. Some notes are from people who knew the soldier (I have left notes for several friends who were killed in Vietnam) and others are general words of appreciation and comfort. I re-read the note I had left on this site for Larry in 2011. It reads, "Every November I fondly remember Larry Betts, my friend in Vietnam who made a lasting impression on me and who was a very good man. I was his RTO when he was killed that day."

To my great surprise, I noticed another note that had been left on this website only a few weeks earlier. I was delighted to see the name on this note, "Ron Berquist." Ron (we all called him Doc) was our medic and a man I knew well from our service together in Vietnam. Ron's message read, "I was his medic. I tried many times to reach his family to tell them exactly what happened with no success." After Larry was hit with fragments from the exploding grenade, Ron was the one who responded to my frantic call, "Medic, Medic!" We both helped the chopper crew load Larry on his final flight to the hospital in Chu Lai. Larry was pronounced DOA (Dead on Arrival); we were shattered by the news of the death of one of our leaders and such a fine man.

Ron had included his email address in his note. I immediately shot off an email to him and within a short time he responded. "Holy Crap, it's great to hear from you. We've all been wondering and asking if anyone had talked to Givens." "What do you mean," I asked. Then Ron explained that since 2010, men from our Company had been gathering together for an annual reunion. These guys most recently met in 2019 over Labor

Day weekend in Nebraska. I asked about my friend, Utah (Roger Brown), who had been my closest friend in training and in Vietnam and who I had not talked with in about forty years. Ron told me that Utah and his wife brought their camper and were present at the Nebraska reunion. Then Ron furnished me a contact list of the men. I left a phone message for Utah (nobody calls him that anymore). I immediately recognized his voice when he called me back. I was elated that we had re-connected. I talked with two other guys from our unit, Greg Klaith and Bob Yantzie. If the Coronavirus doesn't prevent it, I plan to attend the next reunion to be held in Kentucky. There is a lifelong camaraderie between soldiers who were together in Vietnam as we all shared in the life-changing experiences described in this book. What a treat it will be to spend time together and trade war stories with these old friends.

FOOTNOTES

A Note on Sources

This book is a work of nonfiction. It is based primarily on my experiences as a twenty-four-year-old, married, draft-eligible person in the 1960s and my experiences and viewpoints before, during and after serving twelve months in Vietnam. Several of the stories in this book are taken from my first book entitled *Heir to the Kingdom*, published in 2017, generally with some slight changes for clarification, correction, or brevity. In Chapter Eight, I have quoted directly from *Heir to the Kingdom* and so indicated in the appropriate section beginning with "Faith Alive Seminar" and ending with "Spiritual Transformation." Other sources are noted below.

Chapter One

1 American War Library.com/Vietnam/vwafl.htm, *Allied Troop Levels 1960-1973,* Department of Defense, Manpower Data Center.
2 President Eisenhower press conference, April 7, 1954, *"Falling Domino Comment,"* in response to question from Robert Richard.
3 Presidential Papers of John F. Kennedy, President's Office Files, Speech Files. *Inaugural Address,* January 20, 1961.
4 American War Library.com/Vietnam/vwafl.htm, *Allied Troop Levels, 1960-1973.*
5 Hannah McKennett, allthat'sinteresting.com/gulf-of-tonkin, *"Gulf of Tonkin Incident, The Lie That Sparked the War,* September 2019.
6 Sarah Larson, *LBJ's War,* New Yorker.com/culture, September 6, 2017.

7 James Wright, *Enduring Vietnam: An American Generation and Its War,* (New York: Thomas Dunne Books and imprint of St. Martins Press, 2017), 235.

8 James Ebert, *A Life in a Year, The American Infantryman in Vietnam, 1965-1972,* (New York: Random House Publishing Group, 1993), 6

9 Christian Appy, *Working Class War: American Combat Soldiers and Vietnam, 6*

10 Ed. By A.H. Horne, *The Wounded Generation: America After Vietnam* (Englewood Cliffs, NJ: Prentice-Hall, 1981), 10

11 Ebert, *A Life in a Year, The American Infantryman in Vietnam, 1965-1972,* 7.

12 History.com/topics/1960s/watts-riots, August 21, 2018.

13 Tony Briscoe, William Lee and Ese Olumhense, graphics.chicagotribune.com/riots-chicago-1968-mlk.

14 Joel Achenbach, *A Party That Had Lost Its Mind-in-1968, The Washington Post,* washingtonpost.com/news/retropolis/wp/2018/08/24, August 24, 2018.

15 Dan Walker, Committee on the Causes and Prevention of Violence, *Rights in Conflict.* 1969.

16 Stanley Karnow, *Vietnam: A History* (New York: Viking Press, 1983), 598.

17 A.J. Langguth, *Our Vietnam* (New York: Simon & Schuster, 2000), 594.

18 Joe Eszterhas and Michael Roberts, *Thirteen Seconds: Confrontation at Kent State* (Cleveland; Gray and Company Publishers, 1970).

19 Eszterhas and Roberts, *Thirteen Seconds: Confrontation at Kent State.*

20 Archive.org, *1970 Vietnam War Protests in Washington DC May 9, 1970 March on White House,* 49614, July 20, 2017.

21 Self.gutenberg.org/Articles/student_strike_of-1970. Nixon Administration Reaction. Raymond Price, Nixon speechwriter quote.

22 Sasha Cohen, *Time Magazine, The Day Women Went on Strike,* August 26, 2015.

23 Barbara Wulff, *Top 100 Speeches of the 20th Century,* compiled by research from The University of Wisconsin-Madison and A&M University, December 15,1999.

24 Jenni Fink, Newsweek.com/martin-luther-king-jr., *I Have a Dream* speech, January 20, 2020. Reprinted by arrangement with The Heirs to the Estate of Martin Luther King Jr., c/o Writer's House as agent for the proprietor New York, NY. Copyright 1963 by Dr, Martin Luther King Jr. Renewed 1991 by Coretta Scott King.

25 Appy, *Working Class War,* 20.

Chapter Six

1 History.com editors, https://www.history.com, *This Day in History President Carter Pardons Draft Dodgers,* November 24, 2009.
2 Christian Appy, *Working Class War: American Combat Soldiers and Vietnam* (New York: Atlantic Monthly Press, 2011), 37.
3 Appy, *Working Class War: American Combat Soldiers and Vietnam* 37.

Chapter Seven

1 Transcript of Jane Fonda Radio Broadcast from Hanoi, August 22, 1972.
2 History.com editors https://www.history.com *This Day in History President Carter Pardons Draft Dodgers,* November 24, 2009.
3 Ben A. Franklin, *New York Times, President Accepts Vietnam Memorial,* November 12, 1984.
4 Ronald Reagan, *americanrhetoric.com/speeches/ronaldreaganvietnammemorial,* Veteran's Day Ceremony Speech at the Vietnam Veteran's Memorial, delivered November 11, 1988.
5 Jan C. Scruggs and Joel L. Swerdlow, *To Heal A Nation* (New York: Harper and Row Publishers, 1985) 15.
6 Scruggs and Swerdlow, *To Heal A Nation,* 85.
7 Scruggs and Swerdlow, *To Heal A Nation,* 81.
8 Scruggs and Swerdlow, *To Heal A Nation,* 69.
9 Scruggs and Swerdlow, *To Heal A Nation,* 85.
10 Businessinsider.com, *The Greatest Presidents ranked according to political scientists, 2019 and US News Staff, November 6, 2019.*
11 Josephine Minutillo, *ArchitecturalDigest.com,* June 7, 2018.

INDEX OF NAMES AND PLACES

Symbols

3M 202, 203, 207

A

Aden, Norm 18, 77, 78, 156, 169
A.H. Horne 222
Arlington Cemetery 183

B

Bachrach's 207
Badillo and Curry 8
Bangert, Steve xvi
Berquist, Ron (Doc) 68, 151, 219
Betts, Diana (Diana) 76, 77, 78, 155, 156
Betts, Larry (2nd Lt. Betts, Lt.) 73, 74, 78, 111, 155, 219
Betts, Larry III 78, 156
Betts, Larry Jr. (little Larry) 76, 155, 156
Betts, Maddie (Maddie) 78, 156
Betts, Melissa (Melissa) 77, 78, 156
Binh, Long 164, 166
Black Panther Party 14
Bo (interpreter) 74, 75, 149
Boise 77
Bradley, Dave x
Brown County 19
Brown, Roger (Utah) 28, 61, 62, 63, 64, 69, 72, 116, 118, 119, 149, 151, 220
Bush, George W. (President Bush) 7

C

Caldwell, Allyson 196
Caldwell, Jack 196
Caldwell, Sam 196
Cam Ranh Bay 118, 119
Carhart, Tom 184
Carmel 30
Carnahan, Bryden 197
Carswell, Harold 120
Carter, Jimmy (President Carter) 7, 175, 176
Champaign 17
Chicago 10, 16, 18, 151, 168, 169, 222
Colorado Springs 119, 160, 171
Compugraphic Corporation 203
Constitution Mall 183

D

Daley, Richard 10

Decatur xvi, 4, 15, 16, 18, 20, 25, 47, 164, 165, 168, 169, 197
Decatur Club 16
Deffenbaugh, Bob 118
Deffenbaugh, Cindy 118, 159, 189
Dellinger, David 10
Demilitarized Zone (DMZ) 62
Denver 201, 202, 203, 205
Doug (Keller) 54, 198

E

Egert, Alissa 199
Eisenhower, Dwight D. (President Eisenhower) 2, 221
Emogene Cupp 162

F

Father (dad) xvi, 2, 15, 16, 17, 19, 77, 122, 164, 165, 166, 168, 169, 181, 187, 201, 204, 208
Ferguson, Allan (Al) ix
Fletter, Terry 121
Fonda, Jane 175, 223
Fremont 205, 206
Friedan, Betty 12
Ft. Carson 201
Ft. Lauderdale, Florida 16
Ft. Leonard Wood 26
Ft. Ord 26, 30
Ft. Riley 122, 160, 170

G

Gator, Wally 151
General William Peers 114
Germany 170
Givens, Bob (Pvt, Sgt, Sergeant, Robert) xvi, 76
Givens, Charles 169
Givens, Charles (Dad) 15, 17, 122, 164, 165, 166, 168, 201, 204, 208
Givens, Connie (Connie, Connie Richeson) v, xv, 19, 20, 21, 25, 27, 29, 30, 31, 32, 33, 35, 47, 51, 52, 53, 54, 56, 57, 58, 59, 60, 61, 62, 64, 65, 66, 67, 68, 71, 74, 78, 111, 112, 114, 115, 116, 117, 118, 120, 121, 122, 152, 156, 157, 159, 164, 165, 167, 168, 169, 170, 171, 187, 188, 189, 199, 202, 203, 204, 205, 206, 208, 210, 214, 215, 216
Givens, Kierin (Kierin) ix, xv, 195, 196, 199, 202, 206
Glen (Richeson) 19, 53, 168, 199
Goldwater, Barry 6
Gregory, Gary (Gary) 31
Gregory, Jill (Jill) 31
Gulf of Tonkin 5, 6, 8, 221

H

Hartford 20
Harvey Putterbaugh 112
Hayden, Tom 10
Haynes, Bob (Pvt Haynes) 69, 70, 71
Hilton Hawaiian Village 112, 117
Hoa, Bien 61, 62
Ho Chi Minh 175
Honolulu 62, 112, 117
Hope, Bob 114, 115, 119

I

IBM 208, 211
I Corps 62, 64
Indiana University xvi, 18, 19, 53, 202

J

Jesus (Christ) 122, 206, 209, 212, 214, 217
Johnson, Lyndon Baines (President Johnson) 5, 6
Junction City, Kansas 122, 160

K

Keller, Meg 54
Kennedy, Jacqueline Bouvier 3
Kennedy, John F. (President Kennedy) 4, 5, 14, 60, 221
Kent State University 11, 161
Kerry, John 163
Kersten, Pete 210
Kilpatrick, James 184
King, Martin Luther, Jr (MLK) 10, 12, 14
Klaith, Greg 220
Kopecky, Rudy 199

L

Lai, Chu 74, 114, 115, 119, 121, 154, 164, 165, 219
Las Vegas 32, 57, 58, 60
Liberty, Girard 32, 56
Lincoln, Abraham 5
Lin, Maya 183
Livermore 206, 208, 211, 217
LZ Gator 67, 69, 73, 111, 112, 113, 116, 117, 119, 151, 152, 155

M

Malcolm X 14
Marlantes, Karl 161
Marriage Encounter 206, 207
Martin, Dan (Cpt. Martin, Cpt.) 65
Masecchia, Ray 153
McCain, John 184
McCarthy, Dave xiii
McGovern, George 11, 182
Millikin University 4, 15, 17, 47, 197
Mohammed, Elijah 14
Monotype Imaging 198
Monteith, Jim 115, 116
Monterrey 30
Mother (mom) xvi, 16, 17, 52, 53, 77, 168, 169, 170, 189, 201, 202, 206, 211, 214, 215, 216
Mrs. Everett Haith (Shorty) 75, 76, 77
Mrs. Richards 205, 206
My Lai 9, 114

N

NASDAQ 198
Nashville 169, 170, 189, 214, 215
Nebraska City 75, 76
Newton, Huey 14
New York City (New York) 12, 13, 14, 22, 162, 163, 184, 198, 222, 223
Nixon, Richard M. (President Nixon) 9

O

Oakland 210, 211, 213

P

Parry, Jim 21
Parry, Marnie 21
Pat (IBM VP) 32, 208, 209, 211, 212
Payton, Cal 72
Perot, H. Ross 184
Phoenix 76, 77, 78
Price, Ray 12

Q

Quang Ngai Province 74, 119

R

Reagan, Ronald (President Reagan) 176, 179, 180, 181, 186, 223
Reno 58, 60, 208
Rice, Caleb 196
Rice, Dan 196, 199
Rice, Luke 196
Rice, Stephanie (Stephanie) xv, 195, 196, 199, 203
Richeson, Dale 168, 199
Richeson, Dorothy 199
Richeson, Lynette (Lynette) 53, 188, 199, 202
Rock Island, Illinois 19, 25, 51, 61, 195
Rubin, Jerry 10

S

Saigon 9, 61, 164, 165, 175
San Francisco 11, 30, 53, 60, 163, 204, 205, 212
Schmitz, Mary Jane (Mary Jane) 169
Schmitz, Norm 18, 169
School, Dennis 16
Scruggs, Jan C. (Specialist, Spec 4) 181, 182, 183, 184, 185, 186, 191, 223
Seale, Bobby 14
Seattle 164, 168
Sen Charles Mathias 182
Sen Charles Percy 120
Sen John Warner 182
Sgt. Perry (Top) 26, 28, 29, 117, 118, 179, 186, 207, 210, 222
Sgt. Williams (First Sgt. Williams) 65
Shankland, Ralph 168
Shaw, Doug 198
Shimpf, Bill 21
South China Sea 72, 119, 149, 150
South Side Country Club 15
Steinem, Gloria 12
Stevens, Connie 114, 115
Stewart, Norman ix
St. Louis 16, 25, 26
Storrs 20
Sydney 122

T

Tanner, Bill 151
Taylor, Elizabeth 185
Thompson, Carol 30, 53
Travis AFB 59, 60
Tripler Army Medical Center 117

U

University of California (Berkeley) 5
University of Connecticut 20, 202, 207
University of Denver 201, 202
University of Illinois 17, 18, 31
University of Nebraska 73, 76

V

Van Bieber, Leslie 63, 153
Van Zandt, Bob 151, 171
Vietnam Veterans Memorial (Wall, Memorial Wall) 179

W

Washington D.C. (Washington) xv, 11, 12, 35, 162, 164, 181, 182, 183, 191, 192, 222
Watts (L.A.) 9, 222
Willimantic 20, 54

Y

Yantzie, Bob x, 164, 220
Yonan, Emmanuel (Yo) 31, 32

Lightning Source UK Ltd.
Milton Keynes UK
UKHW040653201220
375014UK00024B/771/J

9 781480 895201